PRAISE FOR ∧

THE SHIT NOBODY TELLS YOU ABOUT PARENTHOOD UNTIL IT'S TOO LATE

'Ace – really funny and great writing' – Sam Avery, The Learner Parent

'Brilliant' – Gemma Ray, BBC Radio Lancashire

'Hilarious moments that will strike a chord with mothers everywhere' – The Daily Mail

'So, so funny' – Anouska Williams, BBC Radio Berkshire

'The hilarious life of the unglam Mum...warts and all' – Woman's Own magazine

'You are bang on with everything. You're the first person who has finally said it' – The Hot Mess Mums Podcast

'Funny and frank' – Honest Mum, Vicki Broadbent

'Brutally honest' – Emma Cottam, Positive Wellbeing Podcast for Mums

'The laugh out loud tales are relatable and raw' – The Natural Parenting Magazine

Super funny...it had me in stitches' – Navigating the Motherhood Podcast

MUM'S

THE

WORD 2

REBECCA OXTOBY

For my mum

WHAT A BLOODY GOOD JOB YOU'VE DONE

FOREWORD

Welcome back Mamas (and Dads, Grandmas, Nannies, Grandads, lovely friends who don't want kids but supported the book anyway, oh, and the sadists who just love to read about nipple thrush and mini-meltdowns).

When the last book was released, in May 2020, we were in the midst of a global pandemic. The world was on its arse, and we locked down, in unison, to protect one another. It was a bloody scary time.

I'm writing this book as we step into 2021, and to be honest, I'm bored shitless of Covid-19 now. In work, we're drowning in a second, maybe even third wave (I've lost count) and the country is double-dipping into local lockdowns like nachos in sour cream. At home, we're still not allowed to see family inside the house, but we can see them wherever there is a contactless card machine. I guess the Rona won't catch us there?

Anyway, I've decided that I don't want to talk about it in this book. It's engulfed every aspect of the media for a year, and it's impacted both the physical and the mental health of millions. So, for the few hours that you're reading this book, Covid-19 won't, and never did, exist.

Surviving round two

(I mean, year two)

And just like that, the baby has gone. A tornado toddler has taken her place; a sassy, loud and bipolar little character, with boundless energy and the grip strength of a great white shark. She still shits herself, but now, she has the ability to scarper mid-nappy change, leaving a trail of shitty remnants in her wake. Oh, and all of the home-made, nutritious and wonderfully varied food she indulged in during the weaning phase has now been replaced exclusively by bread and chips, despite the exhaustive efforts of her parents, who are yet to recover from the sleepless nights of the past year.

For when this child now wakes, she will stand at her baby gate and shout jargonistic abuse, whilst shaking the bars like an outraged prisoner. She gives no shits that it's 6.30am, because she has finally slept through for 12 hours, so it's time for this household to get their asses up, whether Mummy and Daddy like it or not.

The teeny little boob-monster is now a walking, talking sass-pot. She wrongly believes that she is independent, yet the only thing that she can successfully accomplish is the ability to turn a four-bedroomed house into a glorified shit-hole within 20 minutes of waking. And yet, she still can't put her own socks on, or wipe her arse.

This book explores the second year of parenthood, and the transition from baby mama to mediator, negotiator, working mother and multi-tasking mother fluffer.

And before we go, just a small announcement for all our guests on board: please remember that I haven't the faintest fuck how to bring a child up. I can't stress enough that this isn't a parenting manual. It's a breakdown on paper with some LOLs along the way, mainly at my husband's expense.

A

ADULTING

Having a child in your house for over a year does something terrifying to your brain. Perhaps it's a combination of unprecedented fatigue, and the relentless numbing of your mind through countless episodes of *Hey Duggee*, but I think I'm becoming a grown-up. I mean, I still have no idea how to do a tax return or purchase stocks or investment bonds, but I've noticed a few strange things happening, like:

- finding myself filled with that scrumptious yet pathetic sense of glee on a windy, dry day, simply because *it's a great day for washing'*. On the mum-o-meter, this is up there with the unease at the thought of *'washing all over the house'* on a rainy Sunday when family spontaneously come to visit.

- being able to sense the contents of an envelope by looking at it, and getting a little giddy feeling at the thought of opening something that I know isn't a bill. Of course, that something turns out to be a birthday card from the *Postcode Lottery*, or a charity inviting you to give a fiver a month to dogs with no legs. Every time I feel that quizzical joy, I grow another crow's foot on my face.

- shamelessly recalling one of my happiest days of the year as the day that I bought a *Shark hoover* – it was genuinely up there with my engagement, the first time Isabelle slept through the night, and the first day of *crème egg* season (1st of Jan FYI).

- buying brand washing up liquid because *'it genuinely does last longer,'* and feeling like the mum on the *Fairy Liquid* advert by draining the contents (though I'm doing this to get my money's worth; nothing to do with wanting to make a rocket with my kid; I might be old but I'm still lazy AF).

- realising that 91% of the photos on my phone are of my daughter, and the rest are screenshots of order confirmations, that I take *'in case I need them'*, but I know that I'll never look at again and will batch delete in 6 months when my storage is full.

- subconsciously lowering the volume of the radio to be able to *'see better'* when driving (I'm convinced that this works).

- wearing my glasses to work every once in a while, to *'give my eyes a rest'*.

- I've even started shamelessly licking my finger to wipe dirt off her face. I'm practically a pensioner.

Unfortunately, the mundanity that comes with being a nearly-adult isn't automatically accompanied by useful grown-up behaviour, like having any sort of inclination to use the washing machine's integrated timer facility, or folding and putting away said washing within less than 5-10 business days. I'm pretty sure that *'the smell test'* of clothes on the bedroom floor isn't how real grown-ups do it, and I'm still at least five years away from meal-prepping like a boss.

I actually find the whole *feeding another person* thing exhausting. What happened to the days when you couldn't be arsed to cook, so just ate whatever was in the treat cupboard until you felt nauseous? It's frowned upon to let your kid eat *Miniature Heroes* and a pack of *McCoy's* for tea (so I've been told) but there are only so many things you can do with frozen chicken nuggets. If we were to do one of those *Eatwell plates* to represent Isabelle's dietary intake, Mr. *Birdseye's* finest delicacies would cover a third, *veg that needs eating* would cover a quarter, and the remainder would be filled by fluff-coated bits from the previous meal that she had found under her highchair. Oops.

If I'm honest, the whole *I'm a mum* thing still overwhelms me. I guess it just doesn't feel real; I mean, my grey hairs and podgy belly would tell you otherwise, but mums are meant to be real grown-ups, with their shit together. They know how to do adult things, like sewing, and they know what all the bits on the hoover are for. They remember everyone's birthdays, and carry stamps and packs of tissues, even if they don't have a cold. I just find it odd that that's meant to be me now. Me; the girl who lost her purse in *M&S* car park because she gave it to a one-year old to occupy her while she paid for seven packs of *Percy Pigs* and a sausage roll.

Danny still says *'can you believe that there is a little person running around the house?'* and the truth is, I can't. I know we longed for her, but it's mental to me that an actual child lives here now. She's not a baby anymore; that teeny little munchkin who sucked my boob and shat through her clothes has gone. She's a kid; with a voice, a mind and a stinking-attitude. And I'm that kid's mum.

AFFECTION

Something pretty spectacular happens in the second year; your snack-hoarding, mess-making, tantrum-taking toddler starts to return affection. Their willingness to do this is surely related to evolution, as it comes just at the time that you start to Google whether 15 months is too early to send a child to boarding school (unfortunately, it is). Isabelle's spontaneous cuddles are delicious; absolutely nothing on this earth compares to that feeling (apart from *Nutella* off a spoon in a candlelit bath. Or nap time). The first time she pursed her little lips to give me an overly-sloppy kiss defrosted my icy heart and reminded me that <u>this</u> is what it is all about. This, unbelievable, infinite love for a teeny person who you grew yourself. Then, they accidentally head-butt you in the chin and normality is restored.

ARMS UP

How cute was that to begin with? Their little *Puss in Boots* eyes staring up at you as they hold their arms into the air for a cuddle. Sadly, it becomes slightly irritating after a while, particularly when you're a 20-minute walk away from home, carrying shopping bags in both hands, or when, from nowhere, they appear beneath your feet, sending you arse over tit into a pile on the floor.

And please don't get me started on their point-blank refusal to put their arms up when undressing them, instead, immediately clamping down their limbs at their side like an army general. People talk about the immense inner strength of a mother rescuing her child from underneath a car, but, I promise, that is negligible when compared to a reluctant toddler 20 minutes before bedtime.

But at least those battles are unwitnessed. There is nothing more cringe-worthy than the child's blunt rejection at the outstretched arms of a well-meaning relative, accompanied by an award-winning resting bitch face; world, just swallow me up, please.

ATTENTION SPAN

Please tell me that I'm not the only one whose child has the attention span of a cognitively-impaired goldfish? It's the reason I've jacked in any form of *sensory play* - it takes 20 minutes to set up, she sits in front of it for 27 seconds and then runs into the kitchen to play with a fucking unwashed spatula. What a waste of my life.

Art and crafts are exactly the same; she mithers to *'draw',* but by the time I've found the pencils and got a bit of A4 out of the printer, she's moved onto entertaining herself by seeing how far a toilet roll can unravel across the landing. For anyone interested, it unravels a fucking lot.

I thought I'd really thrive when it came to educating her, but, as it happens, teaching a one-year old numbers and letters isn't half as enjoyable as I'd imagined. She doesn't even make it to number three before she starts doing swirly woos around the living room whilst chanting a haka, and yet, that irritating cartoon pork can keep her attention for hours.

B

BAG

Remember clutch bags? How about those little over-the-shoulder strappy bags? Or, if you were really cocky with all of your nothingness, you could just carry your card and phone in your pocket? Oh, how the other half live.

Leaving the house with a toddler is like planning for an apocalypse, but you aren't sure which Act of God will be the cause of your ultimate demise. You'll pack three outfits, just in case there is a tsunami (or poonami, puddle, slip in the mud or drink spillage), enough toys to see you through an earthquake, and a corner shop's worth of treats and snacks just in case a tornado toddler needs bribing into submission. I'm pretty much carrying a military backpack just to get me around *ASDA*.

I thought it'd be easier with a toddler. I guess I forgot that they still need all of the baby shit, but now they also want: toys, healthy snacks, water, her chosen teddy of the week, unhealthy snacks in case the healthy ones are rejected, a random part of a toy set that she's grown attached to, and more fucking snacks. And don't tell me that it's easier because you don't need milk; I used to make that on demand like Daisy the Dairy Fairy, so unless I start lactating raisins, it's 1-0 to the baby bag.

BATH TIME

It's probably controversial this, but I can't be the only mother who doesn't bath their kid every day, right? It's such a faff! I appreciate hygiene, honestly, I do, but it seems so counter-intuitive to wash a child and then send them straight back to nursery, only to come home with a matted combination of slime and rice crispies in her hair within 24 hours.

She's now taken to loving the bath too (of course, she plays hard to get and acts like she fucking loathes it until she's in there), so a quick wash is out of the question. The other day she staged a mutiny; point blank refusing to get out of the rather tepid water, resulting in me having to forcibly remove her like a rogue hen at *Popworld*, subsequently prompting shit to hit the fan at 6.30pm. I then spent 15 minutes chasing a now shivering child around the landing, bribing her with anything from teddies to bottles to the empty promises of chocolate and the park in the morning, just to get a nappy back on her bare arse before she ruined my carpet (again). She eventually succumbed, but we were both exhausted, and somehow, the carpet throughout the whole of the upstairs of the house was piss-wet through. So, no, there isn't a hope in hell that I'm doing that again tomorrow, thanks. A bit of dry shampoo and a wet wipe works wonders for us all, you included, Isabelle.

BIG GIRL BED

My baby has officially gone. We moved her out of the cot and into a big girl bed when bedtime became a living hell once more. I have to hand it to her, I was impressed with her nightly core-of-steel crunches in mid-air as she refused to get into the crib, but it was less than convenient in terms of maintaining my sanity, and my marriage.

So we bought a cute little toddler bed and new bedding (including a duvet, which, if you've ever read an actual parenting book is made out to be the single most terrifying thing you could ever put over your child).

She was obsessed with the new bed; either pretending to sleep in it all throughout the day, or tucking her teddies in and kissing them *'goodnight'.* *'Winner'* I thought. That was until bedtime came, when she vehemently refused to sleep without Danny or I by her side. Of course, she would eventually surrender to the *Land of Nod*, and I'd have to sneak out of the room by rolling across the floor like an overweight ninja in Primark pyjamas. My Olympic efforts were in vain though, as, without even opening her eyes, the little freak would sense that I'd scarpered by the sound of my clicky ankles as I stood up at the door.

After weeks of losing my evenings, and subsequently, my mind, I confided in a friend who is absolute #mumgoals. She told me to put her in bed and... just leave.

She acknowledged that it'd be hell, but reminded me that I probably wouldn't want to spend the next 500 evenings of my life pretending to sleep next to a stuffed bear and an incontinent toddler.

So, I did it. I left her.

At the start, I'd tuck her in, and, like clockwork, she would climb straight back out and stand in protest; barricaded into her room by the newly-fitted baby-gate. She would scream cryptic baby jargon as I sat downstairs praying for her to stop, or, at least, for it to not cause lasting psychological harm to either of us.

Eventually, she did fall asleep, but for the first few nights, her defiance bit her on the arse. She became so tired that she fell asleep at the gate, with her little head pushed up against the metal bars. Of course, we moved her (after a few hours, I'm not risking waking a sleeping baby for anybody).

Though I jest, I felt like a shit mother and, even though I was proud of her dogged determination in the face of adversity, I just wanted it to work.

And. It. Did.

After a few uncomfortable nights of carpet burns for her, and a large glass of gin – to drown out the tears – for me, the stubborn little mule fell asleep in her big girl bed, and stayed there all night. I've never been prouder (of her, or myself). Mum 1, Isabelle 0. Smashed it.

Now, I know that this will cause a divide in the hypothetical room. Nobody wants their kids crying out, and I certainly didn't find it easy. So, you do you.

It bloody worked for me and she still likes me, so I'll take that over the nightly chunk-meets-ninja rolls any day.

Thanks Zo. I thought you were mental when you suggested it, but it bloody worked.

BIRTHDAY

Let's get this straight; the kid has absolutely no idea that it's their birthday. They aren't sure why we're tunelessly chanting a song at them, they don't give two shits about the £75 personalised unicorn cake you invested in, and they find that bunch of visitors (who haven't been round since their birth) quite overwhelming.

On the morning of Isabelle's first birthday, despite the pile of enticing presents in the corner, she played with an empty *Jaffa Cake* packet for around half an hour. It was as if she knew that the gifts were actually just 12-18 month baby grows and vests, wrapped individually to make the pile look bigger.

BYE

The word that you say when you've had enough of them arsing about and need to pick up the pace. This may be mid-tantrum in *ASDA* (other supermarkets are available for tantrums, she's done them all), when they won't get their bastard shoes on and you're already running 20 minutes late for a family meal, or when you're out on one of those Insta-worthy family walks and, suddenly, none of their limbs work, so they lie in a heap on the floor and scream bloody murder at the concerned old lady passing by; making you look like a prize prick in a shit-storm.

Ultimately, it's what you say when you don't really know what to do next. It's the bluff you call in a pathetic attempt to get them to sort their shit out and act like a nice person for once in their lives. The problem is, the success rate of the *'bye'* method is low. They're already sick of you imparting health and safety advice - like don't drink the toilet water or lick the cat - so you leaving them free to do as they wish would be an absolute treat.

I'm not going to lie, I'm a novice when it comes to this method. Though I say *'bye'* with conviction, both her and I know that I'm not going anywhere. My authoritative chant is followed by a long, motionless wait as I desperately hope that she moves, because, unfortunately, social services would frown upon me actually bailing from the situation, no matter how tempting it seems. I also couldn't deal with the paperwork of a court case right now.

And yet, I still chant it in anticipation. The Royal We still hopes that, one day, they'll respond with *'oh no Mummy I'm sorry, I got distracted stirring a bit of dog poo with a stick. I'll hurry along immediately'.*

C

Cake smash

Oh, *Pinterest*, you evil genius. A year in, and you still manage to convince me that I can replicate your beautifully-depicted *'do this gorgeous thing at home with your savage one-year old'*. Of course, I'm too tight to pay for a professional cake smash, so I attempted it myself: balloon arch, faux flowers, a wooden *O N E* and the number *1*, a cute unicorn cake from *ASDA* and a little tutu for Isabelle, you know, that kid that LOVES to destroy everything in her path. Surely being allowed to smash up a cake is her ultimate dream, right?

What do you mean she didn't even touch the cake and turned to face the wall for the entirety of the shoot? And the wind kept blowing the balloons away AND she wouldn't let go of the letter *O* and the number *1*, so every photo appears to be celebrating a hobbit's 10th birthday. Absolute fail. At least I didn't pay for the privilege though, hey?

CAR

Oh, how I miss being able to see the footwell of my car. How I long for five functional seats and a boot that can fit more than half a bag of shopping wedged around a pram, spare coat, dirty wellies and a sand-laden blanket. I'm not quite sure if I want to know what the sticky substance is on the back of the driver's seat, or the damage caused by the forgotten apple that rolled beyond my reach in the footwell, three months ago.

Of course, I debated taking it for a valet, but I'm too embarrassed to let anyone see, or smell, inside. I could clean it myself, but I'm afraid that disrupting the rubbish would go against hazardous waste regulations.

So, it just exists this way. This, shit-holey-probably-needs-condemning-stinks-of-rotten-apple kind of way. Each journey, I pray that nothing rolls under my pedals and causes a fatal accident. But, ever the optimist, at least there are left-over snacks on hand to keep the kid quiet.

It's ironic that for the first 12 months, we utilised the car at all ungodly hours, in an attempt to get her to fall asleep, and now, we do everything within our power to prevent a mid-car nap (poking, blasting music, opening all of the windows in the middle of a

January-snowstorm), all because I'm sure as hell not using up my only kid-free hour of the day whilst I'm driving.

CAR SEATS

Wonderful. Not only can I no longer seamlessly transition my sleeping child into the house from the bastard seat, but her brute strength is only growing when it comes to restraining against being fastened into it. She clings on like a petrified koala as soon as I open the damned car door. I'm blown away, and almost proud, that my two stone daughter can match the strength of her eleven stone mother, though admittedly, I don't always show my pride when she's slumping out of the seat, kicking and screaming in a busy car park, all whilst some impatient prick is indicating and tapping on the steering wheel as he waits to get into my space.

Though I am reluctant to give advice (as the old saying goes, *I haven't the faintest fuck what I'm doing*), I will say that snacks are the answer. Well, I'm sure that Karen would argue, and say that discipline, communication and understanding are the real answer, but snacks work too.

Apart from on 22nd March 2021. Snacks didn't work that day, because Isabelle had a little tickly cough, which, when combined with said snacks, resulted in her regurgitating everything she'd eaten that morning into her lap, and onto the car seat.

'Poor child' you may think, but don't worry, she was immediately fine (and that is why nursery will never know the reason that we were 20 minutes late).

What you should be thinking is *'poor mother'*, because if you've ever tried to wash the cover of a car seat, you'll know that I lost two days of my life the moment that those raisins reappeared from her mouth. I'm still not completely sure that I've put it all back together the right way, so if you're driving near me, please keep your distance.

CLIMBING

Why are they so obsessed with climbing? Onto toys, tables, up the loft hatch ladder (unless you're from social services, in which case, this is just a joke). Developmental books will explain climbing as part of the *trajectory schema*, where children like to explore how both they and other objects move. It's also the reason that they throw shit off a highchair (and this will be my explanation to the withered waiter when she launches her lunch at him).

She's started climbing on top of her ride-along car; cockily standing up on the seat and shouting *'get down'* with her arms in the air and a grin on her face. I'd shout at her if I wasn't impressed with her advanced level of sarcasm.

You see, that's the problem with toddlers; they're bloody funny. We've failed to successfully parent on countless occasions, all because of our demon offspring's comedic timing. Danny pisses all over my authority by sniggering behind his hands, as she unwittingly serves up quips like she's an undiscovered talent on the comedy circuit. And, though I'm desperate to hold some sort of order over the house, I'm secretly buzzing that she's already funnier than her Dad.

CLOTHES

The need to buy clothes for them doesn't slow down like I'd expected it to. Though the ages no longer go up every three months, the little monsters still need seasonal dresswear. What a farce.

And, how I wish that I could go back to a time when she couldn't put on her own damn shoes. How do you explain to a one-year old that you can't wear your wellies in bed?

They also need to work on their consistency when it comes to what they want to wear; one minute they're kicking off because you've politely asked them to put their coat on, and 20 minutes later, they point-blank refuse to take it off. Come on, give me a break.

CUTLERY DRAWER

Random, I know, but there is definitely a disparity between my pre-Mum cutlery drawer and this unorganised shit show: half a *Calpol* syringe, multiple, mis-matched bolognese-stained children's spoons, a few of those *Cow & Gate* scoops (in case my personality ever morphed into a mother that enjoys arts and crafts), *Peppa Pig* plasters, three felt tips – all missing their lids – and four forks but no fucking knives. And HOW did all of those crumbs and fluff get in there? In the last book, I ranted about visitors not making their own brews in my house, but please, God, if you're coming any time soon, just bring a flask.

D

DANCING

Is there anything funnier than a toddler spontaneously busting a move? I love the flailing arms and lack of rhythm (she gets that from her dad). I have the most incredible video of her head-banging, in time, to Missy Elliot's *'Work it'*. It's just a shame the lyrics that she's grooving to are *'sex me so good I say blah-blah-blah'*. Not one to share with the grandparents.

I love a good bop with her in the car. I'm actually trying to teach her the words to *Hamilton the*

Musical (ever the optimist). She's not as impressed with my rapping as I thought she'd be though, yesterday she heckled me mid-way through *Satisfied,* shouting *'SHITE' 'SHITE' 'SHITE'.* I was mortified until I realised that she was pointing at the decorative *lights* outside a passing Indian takeaway.

She's started requesting music on the TV, namely *'Dumble'.* You know, the irritating clown whose fake laugh makes me want to cut my own ears off and send them to him in the post. I'm telling you now, Isabelle, I will disown you if you ever *'wiggle your bottom, shake and grin'* for a man. *Robert the Robot,* on the other hand, could dust for me any day.

I'm ashamed to admit that despite my hatred for these 21st century hip nursery rhymes, I've found myself mum-bopping along to them. Have you heard *Little Baby Bum's* version of *This Old Man?* The old guy's jazz solo is something else. It's an absolute tune.

Sadly, the same can't be said for *5 Little Monkeys*. that GP should have reported Mummy monkey after the second kid fell off the bed (not the first, we've all been there), but now she's got five with head injuries and not once have the social been round.

I'm also not down with *10 in the bed*. Three is a bloody crowd. It's amazing how fucking massive a toddler can make themselves when the lights go off (and no, Karen, she doesn't sleep in our bed, she jumps in in the morning for cuddles and the occasional head-butt – her to me, not the other way around).

DISCIPLINE

As the little buggers actually transform into mini people, you have to step up your parenting game to instil some sort of authority (apparently). This involves deciding how to discipline the child, and finding a suitable response to them launching pesto pasta off their highchair, or licking a dog, for example.

You see, I'm the perfect *Hypothetical Mum*. In *Hypothetical Mum World*, I'd get down on her level and calmly explain to her that if she sucks on my make-up brush, not only will it taste yucky because it is full of germies (and I mean *full;* I haven't cleaned them for years), but it will also make Mummy sad, because it's the only thing that stops people from looking at her face and doing that pity head-tilt thing, because they think that she's terminally ill.

The problem is, I don't live in *Hypothetical Mum World.* I live in Warrington, a little town between Liverpool and Manchester. And in Warrington, it takes 25 minutes to dress a one-year old, because she thinks its fucking hilarious to run around the landing slapping her belly and shouting *'wit woo'.* In

Warrington, that same toddler screams bloody murder if I stop her from playing with a razor or sucking the bleach off a toilet brush. (Oh, and Warrington is also home to the first UK *IKEA*, fact fans).

Now, this is where the readers are divided into the *Hypothetical Mum Mafia* (AKA Karen) and *Team Tired* (captained by me). The Karens will say *'how on Earth could you leave a child within reach of a razor?'*. Good question, Karen, I haven't shaved my legs for months, but shit happens (and, incidentally, that's what the toilet brush is for).

I'm trying with all my might to instil some level of respect in her, but she just takes the piss out of me. I even attempted my mother's tried and tested *'countdown from five'* approach. That terrified me when I was a kid, but Isabellend just counts backwards along with me, throwing her head from side to side like an impudent little cow. I can't deny that I'm impressed with her numeracy skills, but her attitude makes me want to wallop her. Her no-shit response called my bluff, as I don't actually know what's meant to happen when you get to *one*; I only ever got to *two* before I crapped myself when I was on the receiving end. So, I just start counting slower, with pleads of compliance between each number like the desperate, broken woman I am.

DOORS

Question: How fascinating are doors?

Answer: not very, unless you're my joiner husband or my daredevil daughter. She's obsessed with opening and closing doors, saying *'door'* and sticking her little fingers in that lovely little gap between the door and the frame (then again, so is he, to be honest). I don't know how many times you have to shout *'watch your fingers'* before they actually watch them, but 23534 isn't enough, apparently.

Her love for doors extends to those beyond our home. She particularly likes testing the door handles of public toilets, specifically during that sacred time about three seconds after Mummy has just sat down for a piss, and is now mid-flow with a sub-optimal pelvic floor. Pants around my ankles, I furiously waddle over to stop her from grabbing the enormous lever of the baby changing room door handle, just as she grasps it and reveals my bare backside and semi-continent vagina to my awaiting public. To top it off, she then tries to make a run for it; cue a half-naked 30 year old, chasing her giggling child around *Starbucks* like a Roly Poly stripper in a *Benny Hill* sketch. Thanks, Izzy.

DUST

Yes, my house is a shithole. I can't keep up. I'll try to tidy, and occasionally clean the bits we can all see, but Jesus wept, have you ever looked behind your bed? We're currently in the final development stages of a dust mites' version of the *Atlantis The Palm* hotel down there, and don't even get me started on underneath the non-slip mat in the bath (if you've got one of these, put the book down and go and look underneath it; it'll make me feel better knowing that you're a scumbag too).

A few weeks back, I crept into a sleeping Isabelle's bedroom to investigate *the case of the flying insect* that I could see roaming around her bedroom on the baby monitor. As it happens, it was just insect-sized dust particles floating across the lens.

But there is nothing more soul-crushing than the fingerprints. Her dad (thanks Danny) has taken to letting her wave from the window as one of us is leaving the house, which is usually straight after her breakfast. As a result, our previously transparent window panes are now barely translucent; marked with smeared handprints of milk and cornflakes and banana slime, like a toddler's vile re-enactment of that steamy scene in *Titanic*.

Of course, my mum friends always come up trumps in this situation, providing me with all of the comfort I need in knowing that I'm not the only scrubber out there. My wonderful friend, Becs (shoutout @jugglewear) messaged me to say that she once sat blissfully enjoying a brew whilst her son chased a disgustingly large ball of fluff around the kitchen, which had crawled out from under the fridge. These are the mums that we need in our lives.

And though I joke, my head and my heart have a constant battle around the topic of having a cleaner.

I came from a single parent household; my mum worked full-time and our house was always spotless, so I feel like I can't excuse any inability to keep up with the housework when I have a partner at home and one less child, though the partner does heavily contribute to the shit-hole vibes.

I also feel as though I would clean up before the cleaner came, which kind of defeats the point. Perhaps I could pretend that I had a cleaner who was on her way, and that way, I'd be motivated to sort my shit out, because we all know that nothing moves quicker than a mother in a dirty house with a visitor on the way.

E

Eating Out

Going to restaurants is one of my favourite things to do. Even though I'm ridiculously fussy and always pick the same thing – rump steak, medium-well (calm down, Karen) and mushy peas – I hate cooking, and double-hate washing up. When we had Isabelle, I was convinced that I'd continue to eat out, and she would be one of those children who would happily colour-in whilst waiting for her nutritious children's meal; which she would eat peacefully, with no mess, as we discussed our favourite part of the day.

Oh, bless my innocence.

I do still take her out for a meal, and whilst she likes to chew on those highly-contaminated colouring pencils, before launching them off the highchair and onto the floor, she certainly doesn't sit quietly. And though I'm far from an advocate for *'children should be seen and not heard'*, I draw the line at her bellowing *'OY YOU'* at strangers, in an attempt to persuade them to share their food with her. She also, at any given moment, can decide to break free from the highchair and feign rigor mortis as I quietly, and desperately, attempt to restrain her back into the seat. Every bribe from my bag of tricks is scattered across the floor before the starters have even arrived (what kind of cocky shit orders starters with a one-year old?) and shit will literally hit the fan if we have to wait for the bill. I've often walked her to and from the toilet seven times before it arrives, with its cocky little smiley face signature as if they hadn't caused a full meltdown of both a toddler and her 30-something mother.

I'm going to have to resort to microwave meals off paper plates for the next 17 years, aren't I?

ENERGY

These miniature humans have boundless energy. I can't keep up. Her enthusiasm and zest for life is adorable; the way she bounces into our bedroom (at 5.40am) and giggles just because she has seen her Daddy's face. The way she rediscovers her toys each day, and does a happy dance when she gets a snack.

What's not so cute is the way she legs it up and down the aisles of *ASDA*, forcing me to run after her with a trolley like I'm a withered contestant on

Supermarket Sweep. It's also less than adorable when she decides to climb the slide the wrong way in the park, so I look like a prick doing that awkward *'excuse me, sorry'* shuffle passed the other parents to get her down, before she falls to her inevitable death and makes a holy show of me.

Of course, the burning ball of energy will eventually combust, leaving an overtired shell of a child in its place. If you have impeccable timing, you'd be arriving home just at this moment, to lead the child straight up the stairs and to bed for a nap. Usually, however, the demon toddler arrives just as you're answering an important phone call, entering a supermarket, or visiting a relative. The result?

Hell on earth.

Expert status

It's funny how quickly the novice becomes the expert in *Mum World*. Since Isabelle was born, lots of my friends have become mothers for the first time, and somehow, they seem to think that I know what I'm doing. That's their first mistake.

I'm not a good friend to a new mother. I really wanted to be, but as it happens, *Toddlergeddon* makes caring for a newborn baby look like a walk in the fucking park.

I know they're knackered, God, we all know that that exhaustion is a son of a bitch, but I can't help thinking *'yeah, but at least your kid stays still'.*

I'm even worse to pregnant women. When they complain that they're tired (because, genuinely, pregnancy is a bitch with exhaustion, pelvic girdle pain, hyperemesis and the rest) all I can think is *'Hun, you've got no fucking idea'.* I stop short of saying it to them, because I'm not a dick, but my sympathetic smile in response to their complaints of tiredness is about as sincere as a politician at a food bank.

F

Farmyard Animals

What a mind fuck; despite never having been asked the sound of a cow in an interview, a quiz show or an A-level exam, we insist on spending hours and hours of our lives aimlessly teaching our children the noises of farmyard animals. And the noises we teach aren't even right: a sheep doesn't say *'baa'*, and a pig definitely doesn't say *'oink'*. It's bullshit. And yet, here I am, alongside every other mother doing a celebratory internal *'whoop whoop'* whenever she impersonates a fucking chicken.

The kid is getting too cocky now, though; last night she argued with me for a good five minutes that a zebra was a *'horsey'*. I probably should have stayed calm and explained that *'whilst they look similar, a zebra is identified by its black and white stripes, which differentiate it from horses which tend to be brown in colour'.* I definitely shouldn't have said, *'no it's a zebra, it's a zebra, no, that's a horse, that's a zebra. No. No, it's a zebra. Fine, it's a fucking horse'.*

FAVOURITE

There is going to come a time when your little darling shows a preference for one of their parents. And, though the cuddles are bloody glorious, there is always a silver lining when their favourite isn't you. Like at 5am, for example. Sorry Daddy, but she's shouting for you, Hun. Get your arse out of bed and close the bedroom door on the way out.

I would be lying if I said that it wasn't an absolute privilege when you *are* the favourite, even if the leg-clinging and whining does get slightly laborious. There is something pretty damn wonderful about them lifting their arms up just for you. In fact, I still can't get my head around it. I'm everything to her. I'm her rock, her comfort, her home. I'm her Mum, and though I don't feel qualified in the slightest, she thinks I'm pretty awesome, and that is my greatest achievement of them all.

Of course, favourites aren't just limited to Mummy and Daddy. Any new mother will eventually realise that they majorly fucked up by not buying two of everything, because inevitably, their child will develop an unhealthy relationship with one particular teddy. If said teddy goes missing, you're screwed for all eternity. For a long while, Isabelle's was a toddler-sized Mickey Mouse, which wasn't easy to lose, but wasn't practical to take anywhere. Of course, it also stunk, prompting the need for a stealth-wash operation when she was either sleeping or in nursery. As if I didn't have enough joy in my life.

FOOD

Is everyone still doing the homemade, nutritious meals, exquisitely presented on a *Bamboo Bamboo* plate?

No?

Oh, good, me neither. I still use the plate because she can't launch it on the floor, but it's mainly filled with beigeness, and I definitely haven't cut her chicken nuggets into fucking unicorns. I'm so tempted to make the Insta account

@whatmummyreallymakes to showcase my culinary talents in all their sub-optimally wholesome glory.

Every mama enters *Mumdom* with the best intentions of only giving their kid delicious, nutritious and home-cooked meals, morning, noon and night. On the rare occasion that they'd express hunger between mealtimes, they'd joyfully snack on crudités and sip water (and only water) from *Nuby360's* premium range, made only of the finest crystal.

Hmm.

This is a tough one. I still want to be *that Mum*. I still want her body to be a temple, that houses only the finest ingredients, but, well, fish fingers are easier, aren't they? I hate cooking, especially if it takes me 45 minutes to prepare a meal that is ultimately going to be smeared into the carpet for me to have to pick out at a later date. I just can't be arsed with the faff, and I know that I should care more, but I've come to terms with it now, and so should you.

FML

At least once a day I mutter *fuck my life* under my breath. It's not that I don't love being a mum, but sometimes, I just have to question what the hell my world has become.

Yesterday, I was drying Isabelle's hair with the hairdryer, when out of nowhere, she licked the hot end. I'm not sure if you've ever licked the hot end of a hairdryer, but it burns like the arse end of hell. She freaked out and cried for about 20 minutes, and despite it being a moronic, self-inflicted injury, she was absolutely furious with me. FML. She won't do that again.

I spent my 30th birthday dancing to *Mr Tumble*'s party playlist (against my will), wearing a plastic hat, in my living room. Whenever I went to sit down, Isabelle would demand that I *'dance'*, like a pimp in a sleazy nightclub. FML. It's a far cry from the water villa in the Maldives that I'd imagined for my big birthday.

She's also recently taken to minesweeping mine and Danny's drinks that we had left out in the living room from the previous night. She definitely has never, ever supped on the dregs of a pinot grigio, I swear.

But, of all the daily FMLs, there is nothing more soul-destroying than having a Mexican stand off with a toddler, pleading with them incessantly just to hurry the fuck up and get into the car, because it's just started pissing with rain and nobody wants to see the world's worst impromptu wet t-shirt competition.

I used to be a strong, independent woman, and now, I'm a self-inflicted snack bitch, living at the mercy of a small child's temper tantrums.

G

Gates

Everything changes when you become a parent; even the previously unremarkable ability to walk from one room into another without tripping over, or stubbing your bastard toe on, a baby-gate. I've got three (baby gates, not toes). Three fluffing gates to pass through, just to get her from the couch to her bed. It's like *Fort Knox* without the gold.

Obviously, there are certain qualities in a baby gate that you don't know that you need to know about until you've bought one. Like the fact that that hideous metal bar across the bottom isn't always a feature, so you could, in fact, have massively reduced your risk of a foot fracture if you'd have just shopped beyond the latest supermarket *Baby Event*. There's a reason they were £4.99 – because no fucker wants them. It's clearly a flawed design to put a metal trip hazard across the length of both the top and bottom stair in the house, as if some prick thought '*Oh, they think they've mastered stairs with a child now? Let's throw two potentially deathly trip hazards up and see how they fare'*. I'm not sure who made them, but I'll tell you now, <u>he</u> didn't have kids.

I thought I'd learnt the error of my ways with the first two gates, so splashed out, at the toy store that rhymes with Biffs, and got myself a fancy £20 jobby. No screws, extendable – so it fits any doorframe – and most importantly, no toe-crushing bar. Of course, I had to make a sacrifice somewhere: I can't open the fucking thing. Every time you want to unlock it you've got to flick the triangle to the side and then pull up the gate, all whilst carrying; a toddler, her toy of choice, a bottle (calm down, Karen, I'm not in the mood) and obviously, my phone. I've jammed my finger in it more times than I ever stubbed my toe, and have had to resort to the fucking high jump just to get back out of her bedroom. And let me tell you now, it's nigh on impossible to sneak out of a sleeping child's room by doing the *Frosby Flop* onto the landing.

I'm desperate to reduce the number of baby gates in my life, but there isn't one that I could confidently remove without dire consequences. If I get rid of the one at the top of the stairs, she will inevitably plummet to her death, and let's be honest, that's less than ideal when I've got another book planned. The one on her bedroom stops her from bolting around the landing, and more importantly, from suddenly appearing at my bedside in the middle of the night like Samara from *The Ring.* And you'd think that the importance of the one on the bottom of the stairs would need no explaining, but, just in case her father is reading this:

It's important to close that gate because she will stealth-climb the stairs within seconds, and then attempt to parkour jump from the top.

So, remember to shut it for God's sake.

(and if you are reading this, put the kettle on, I'm parched).

GUILT

Mum guilt is real. Trust me, I know. It's there whenever she stays over at her grandparents, whenever I pick her up a little bit later at nursery or when I look forward to a day in work, just to get to piss in peace and talk about a patient that isn't *Miss Polly's* sick dolly.

I've cried for a break and cried because I miss her on the exact same day. I've wondered whether I'm working too much, and too little.

I thought it would be easier this year; that the structure of an almost full-time job would mean that I would savour every moment with her outside of work, and that I'd never want time for just me because I'd be too busy to crave it. I thought that there wouldn't be enough hours in the day for me to need space. And yet, here I am, longing for a day alone – to do the pathetic things like clean the fluff tray in the tumble dryer, or finally weed the path. And every time I feel it, I hate myself for craving mundanity over playtime with my girl.

In fact, no, I don't hate me. I hate society for it. I hate the pressure that mums are forced to feel. After the release of the first book, it was reviewed by a lovely little book club called *Bookscape books*. The club has a *WhatsApp* review group and I was an undercover member, because who are more honest than a group of girls in a *WhatsApp* group? The majority gave incredible reviews, but one girl said that I *'should be grateful'* and she felt like I had *'nothing nice to say'* about Isabelle. It hurt like hell. I don't care if you think the book is shit (well, maybe I do a bit) but the suggestion that mothers need to constantly, endlessly and infinitely feel overjoyed about their position as Mum is toxic. Especially coming from another mother.

I'll say it again for the ones at the back, I fucking love my daughter. More than life itself. I am obsessed with her. I'm the one who constantly speaks empty thoughts about her just so that people know that she's mine. Saying that she is my world simply isn't enough. But implying that a mother isn't grateful for the blessing of a child, when she's already tortured by her own twisted, layered and overwhelming mum guilt, is not only a huge *hoorah* to the outdated views of our patriarchal society, it's just fucking mean.

If we can't get over our own mum guilt, let's at least try and snap one another out of it.

H

HACKS

OK, so I'm a parenting legend. Well, not exactly, but I've curated a lovely little list of parenting hacks that will save your sanity in those dark hours. Think *Five Minute Mum*, but without the benefits to the child's development:

- Cut eyes and a mouth hole in a head-sized box. Stick it on your head and ask your child to *'feed the monster chocolate'.* You get sugar and they get entertainment. Voila, I'm a genius.

- When requiring just five minutes of peace, piss or poo, hide a toy in your pocket and send your precious little one to look for it, in another room.
- Blow up a balloon and let it go. Your kid will love chasing after your spit-filled receptacle, and bringing it back to you, like a dog playing *fetch.*
- Blend a packet of *Cheerios* and let your kid play in the *sand* with their animals. Yes, it makes a fucking mess, but it keeps them entertained for long enough to silently scoff a *crème egg* in the kitchen without the inconvenience of them consuming toxic waste in the room next door.
- Publicly announce to the room when you need a wee, and then go. Your declaration is the verbal agreement with your husband that, for the next three minutes, you are not responsible if the child causes serious harm or death to themselves, or your husband.
- If your little one has a rocking horse, place it right in front of the telly, search for *'jockey cam'* on *Youtube* and let them race in the *Grand*

National. Ten whole minutes of peace. For optional, extra Mum-points, pop on a fascinator and cheer them on from the stalls.

- Toddlers love putting stuff in the bin (my car keys, Daddy's toothbrush) so utilise this by unwrapping a tin of miniature heroes and asking your child to put the wrappers in the bin, one by one. To save wastage, you'll have to eat the chocolate, too. Sorry.

HAIR

Question: how can you identify a one-year old in a line up? The broken speech that only a mother can understand? The inability to jump? Or that awful, Bojo pixie cut?

Answer: all of the above. The first two are adorable, but the hair is getting beyond a joke. It's totally unmanageable. She looks like Einstein and Boris Johnson's love child. It's long enough to give off a homeless vibe, but not yet at a length that constitutes a sociably-acceptable style. When it's *down* it looks like a mullet, but she will only leave bobbles in for just long enough to style it into unmanageable quiffy spikes, like Angelica's ugly-ass doll, Cynthia, from the *Rugrats* (google it, Millennials).

I can't cut it; that'll just prolong the current shit show. So, every day, I wet it like a 90s gel-head, and pray it'll tame until she's at nursery and no longer my issue.

My hair isn't much better, I must have been too sleep-deprived to notice the post-partum hair loss in the first year, but the post-partum hair growth is a bitch. Even a year on, I'm rocking the troll-like tufts. Oh, to be Daddy in all of this.

HIDE AND SEEK

Isabelle and I play this every-day. My purse, Daddy's work phone, a shoe, her dirty nappy, the rest of her sandwich: she's an absolute pro. The problem is, I don't want to play, particularly at 6.45am when I'm trying to get a toddler, a husband and myself out of the house. Last week I found my car keys in the door of the fridge, and a pair of Danny's unwashed boxer shorts in my work bag. Cue an unwanted and embarrassing conversation with my colleagues as I pulled those out with my lunchbox, like a horny schoolkid with their first crush.

When it comes to playing hiding games with Isabelle, she's still thriving off of *'Peepo'*, announcing it to the room whenever she appears from behind the door, a curtain or her vest. It's not a surprise to me, Hun, I'm the one putting the vest over your head, because you still can't dress yourself. Do you know that a piglet can walk as soon as it's born? Baby turtles can speak to each other before they even hatch, and a baby seal can swim almost immediately after birth. And yet, my almost two-year old kid still can't put her own socks on.

I

ILL

Fuck. Me.

Being unwell with a toddler is awful. I don't think I ever appreciated how fortunate I was to be poorly without a kid; to just lie in your own filth and fester in front of the TV, without a care in the world. Now, the mum guilt hits you right in the guts, and it's bloody horrible.

That nasty pang in your tummy, knowing that you should be playing with them, but instead you're lying uselessly on the couch; without the energy or the inclination to move anything beyond your fingers on the remote control. The guilt you feel in sabotaging their tiny minds with back to back *Bing*, just so that they don't move or speak to you.

When Isabelle was 18 months old, I suffered the worst migraine I'd had in ages. I remember lying on the couch just wanting to die. My gorgeous little girl tucked me in and gave me her favourite teddy to cuddle, saying *'shh, night night Mummy'.* Of course, I cried my eyes out.

There is no time where you feel more vulnerable than in that moment; knowing that you should be doing more. I kept sending her into the kitchen to get herself a snack, conscious that I'd have to rely on *Ella* and her kitchen to provide all of the sustenance until Daddy came home.

Those days are the longest of days, and though the kid will never, ever remember *the day that Mummy lay on the couch*, it's burnt into my memory as the day I definitely wasn't enough.

Independence

'Here's to strong women; may we know them, may we be them, may we raise them'.

Apart from when we're running 15 minutes late for swimming and she's adamant that she can put her own leggings on (she can't). Or when she wants to drink from her special big girl cup and repeatedly pours it down her front. And I'm not mad on the independence that comes with brushing her own teeth, or wiping her own shitty bum bum.

At 18 months, Isabelle started saying *'Abelle do it'* to just about every activity we did together; painting, drawing, zipping up her coat, putting her bastard wellies on. And I foolishly wanted to raise a strong, independent woman who will fight you to the death if you try to take away her liberties, so everything takes five times longer than if I just did it myself. But, feminism and all that...

INSTAGRAM VS REALITY

Absolute kudos to the mothers who take their kids out for a *Babyccino*. I tried this once with a friend of mine and her son, who is the same age as Isabelle. It resulted in one child fisting their drink, and the other having a full-blown meltdown because I wouldn't let her independently hold a porcelain cup of boiling milk.

Who are these women who 'casually' take insta-perfect pics of their bath set-up? Don't tell me I'm the only one who bathes with a highly-contaminated plastic hippo toy, staring creepily at me from between the empty shampoo bottles that didn't quite make it to the bin?

I don't want to be a dick either, but we need to talk about *'Hinching'* our homes. Who are the mothers who own those labelled bottles? Who are you? I know that it looks pretty, but who the fuck has the time to decant soap into a bottle that says *'soap'?* You already know it's fucking soap. I'm not pouring fabric softener into a rose gold topped *'fabric softener'* glass, I hardly get around to pouring it into the bastard washing machine. And I have no respect for the people who pour cereal into glass jars. If that's you, I'm sorry, I just don't trust you.

J

JUGGLE

The struggle to juggle life as a parent is something else. It's more tangible than I ever thought possible, and I feel the pressure of never really being good enough, wrapping around me most days.

Today, for example, I've worn the following (hypothetical) hats (and I don't even suit fucking hats):

- Mummy
- Wife

- Manager
- Speech and Language Therapist
- Supervisor
- Chef (I'd defo suit a hypothetical chef's hat)
- Cleaner
- Author
- Chauffeur
- Colleague
- Dot Cotton (I'm pretty sure that I'm working in a fucking laundrette)
- Friend
- Daughter
- Sister
- Granddaughter
- Daughter-in-law
- Life administrator
- Only person to put the toothbrushes back in the holder
- Dish-washer emptier
- Bex; whoever she is

This is where Supernanny fucked me over. I genuinely watched that programme, thought that the parents were scum and that my children would be completely different. I believed that their issues with behaviour were all because the parents were too damn lazy to keep tabs on their kids.

In my *Hypothetical Mum* head, I genuinely thought that I would have my eyes on my daughter 24/7 and that I'd be able to dedicate all of my time to her development, entertainment and learning. I based this hilariously naïve notion purely on my previous experience with kids. I'd looked after plenty before, and was perfectly capable of sitting with them for 24 hours until their parents returned. Sometimes, we even did fun things, like paint, build dens or bake cakes. Sometimes, we did all of those things in one day. Hypothetical parenting was a piece of piss.

Because, what they don't tell you when you're promoted from babysitter to parent, is that the kid is no longer your only job.

As a babysitter, you didn't wash a plate, didn't have work uniforms to iron, and certainly didn't give two shits about the mess, because you'd be able to tidy it up when they'd gone.

That's the difference, sweetheart. This isn't babysitting. The kid NEVER LEAVES. So, with all good intentions, you can't sit with them every second of the day, because nobody would ever feed you, and you'd run out of those huge, no VPL knickers that you like within three days. At some point, you have to half-attempt to tidy with the kid in the vicinity; listening out for them being too loud (or more worryingly, too quiet) and checking in on them every once in a while, to make sure that they hadn't blown themselves up.

Now, she hasn't done that (yet). But, I did walk onto the landing mid-bathroom clean to find her half-way up the loft ladder. My life, and hers, flashed before my eyes.

I'm trying so fucking hard to be the best at all the jobs, but feel like I'm not really mastering any of them.

I don't think I have the balance right. I don't know if I ever will. I guess I just feel like I never really tick anything off on the *To Do list of life*. Only now have I realised that it's a completely unattainable goal, because there will always be more patients in work, more washing at home, and more learning and development opportunities for Isabelle than I could ever try to quantify.

It's probably been the hardest life shift for me to come to terms with. Last year, I was at home on maternity leave, so life admin and household chores were achievable during nap times (whether I did them or not is a story for another book…literally). Now, I'm home at 5.30pm at the earliest, and then my second full-time job commences. I'm fortunate; I have Danny and a great family support network. But it's still not easy. In fact, it's fucking difficult. I know I'm beyond hard to please, but I'm living in a cycle of never feeling good enough at work or at home. I wish I could buy more hours in the day. I wish I could stop time just so that I could clean in the hours that didn't matter. I wish I could be the mum who does it all, or even just the one who is satisfied with just one single element of what she's achieved in this manic juggling act.

I'm not crying, you are.

JUMP

Fancy a giggle? Ask your one-year old to jump. Hours of entertainment.

Of course, that is in a controlled environment. It's definitely not as humorous when the little buggers delightedly shout *'JUMP!'* and just fucking launch themselves off high places, with some serious confidence in your ability to leap across the room and catch them.

K

KISSES

Ooh, I just love a toddler kiss (and by toddler, I mean solely *my* toddler; I'm not a creep, and other kids' saliva definitely isn't my bag).

Yeah, her kisses are wetter than I'd usually go for, but they're bloody gorgeous. Her pre-kiss pout would give a trout a run for its money (do fish carry currency?) and the little lip smack noise she makes is just adorable.

(I'm conscious that I'm being one of *those mothers* in this paragraph, but I just really love her – take note book club reviewers).

I'm definitely a *kissy mum*. I didn't think that I would be, God, my poor husband hasn't had a kiss since 2015, but I can't keep my lips off this little madam.

I'm trying to empower her at an early age, by teaching her that she has the freedom to refuse to kiss anyone that she doesn't want to. I try really hard to not tell her to kiss family members or friends, and always ask her if she would like to give me or her dad a kiss. Look at me smashing parenthood.

The problem is, I really want a kiss, and it breaks my heart when she says 'no Mummy'. I'm definitely not saying that I've had a little cry when she rejects my offer, and definitely, definitely, haven't ever bribed her with a biscuit in exchange for a little peck. I've tortured myself over it, but, you know what, a kiss for her mother is different to a random snog in the street; I let her live inside me, rent-free for 9 months. Surely that's worth something?

L

LIBIDO

If you're of a nervous disposition, or a relative, please God, just skip to the next chapter.

You see, it's a funny old thing, having a kid. We all know how it starts – you know – *the deed*. The coming together of two people in the heat of the moment; sharing love, desire and bodily fluids. A passion so intense that it actually has the power to create life.

And then the kid arrives, and your libido falls off the face of the planet. It's either ironic as hell, or your body's subliminal chastity belt, worn solely to protect you from the hell of further pro-creation.

It's as if that part of me died on the day I became a mum, perhaps they removed it with the placenta, and the only way I'd get it back is by paying a hippie to encapsulate it and send it back to me in little pills? (Hold on, is that what lady Viagra is?)

I reckon I know exactly why the horn has vanished; I don't recognise this body anymore, and I definitely don't fancy seeing any extra jiggling of my jiggly bits. I know that Mamas are sexy as hell – there is nothing more incredible than a woman's body – but I still haven't figured out where I fit into this one yet.

Maybe it's nothing to do with my mum-tum? Maybe it's because I'm knackered; I'm juggling a job, a house, a career as an author, a couple of masters modules, friendships, a marriage, oh, and I have to keep a small human alive. How anybody finds the time or energy to rumpy pump is beyond me.

But truthfully, I think the reason for my stalled sex drive is because I'm a mum now. Those nipples fed a child, and if you touch them, you'll activate a nipple-shaped teleportation device, and I'll be transported right back to the moment when I had to juice myself, for six months, just to keep another person alive. Surprisingly, that's not a turn on.

Oh, and also, that scar down there still feels partially numb, like that limp feeling that you get when you've slept on your arm (you men will know what I'm on about). Just the thought of touching that part of my body makes me queasy.

And let's be honest, all that sexy stuff isn't the best use of my time; I could have got a washload on.

I do sometimes wonder if it'll ever come back. Maybe Danny needs to change his tact? Kissing is so out-dated. I reckon the old fire would ignite again immediately if he just remembered to put the bins out.

Locks

The need to child-proof your home comes around quicker than you'd expect. I knew about, and had accepted, the need for baby gates, but I genuinely thought that I'd dodged a bullet when it came to the kitchen cupboards. I'd purposely selected handle-free door fronts, with the naïve aim of preventing small fingers from getting hold of the bleach, or, more importantly, our booze stash. But, my cocky, smart-arsed idea was short-lived, as she mastered opening the doors as soon as she could walk. I'm talking *within minutes.* She's even figured out the fancy corner ones, which is more than can be said for my joiner husband, who has never managed to fully close a cupboard door in his life.

So, now we've had to resort to those ugly, plastic sticky things on all of the doors. The great news is that they prevent her from finding and wielding a nine inch knife around the kitchen, but the bad news is that it now takes me around 25 minutes, three fingernails, two meltdowns and at least twelve expletives just to make a brew.

M

MENTAL HEALTH

Ok, here it is, the deep stuff. It didn't make the first book – the topic is hardly crammed with funny anecdotes, I know – but I think the real reason that I excluded the shittiest bits of my new Mum journey was because I wasn't ready to accept that it was happening. I couldn't stand the idea that I had struggled.

But, you know me now, and I wouldn't be true to you or myself if I didn't bring this little gemstone up. So here we go.

It's pretty tough, motherhood, isn't it? Even for a woman who, on the outside, looks like she's got her shit not only together, but tied up in a gift box with a pretty bow. To quote the great philosophers of *Love Island 2017*, *'on paper'*, my life is perfect.

And somehow, I found myself with post-natal depression; questioning my marriage, my life choices, and my happiness. I was miserable, and whilst I didn't doubt my love for her, I'd be lying if I didn't say that I had pangs of regret, emptiness and misery like I'd never felt before.

It's a bit of a mind fuck to feel lonely and crave being alone at the same time. It's more of a mind fuck to know that everything I'd achieved – personally, professionally and other – is what society tells you is absolute #lifegoals and I still wasn't satisfied.

So, why was I miserable? Why did I need counselling and medication, just to get through the week? Why the fuck, when I had a perfect, healthy and happy little girl, a big house, a nice car, a loving family and a gorgeous husband, was I not *'living my best life'?*

I'd say I don't know, but I do, of course I do.

Your life flips on its head when you become a mum – the world as we know it falls out through your arse (or, more anatomically, your front bum) and you become the single most important thing in the life of a vulnerable, needy and helpless little person. It's all-encompassing, it's suffocating and it's relentless. And when the visitors die down and the novelty of your new addition wears off for the rest of the world, you are left holding the baby. You.

The world tells you to be eternally grateful, happy, and overjoyed with this prospect. They literally tell you that you must *'enjoy every moment because it goes too fast',* but nobody tells you that it's fine to grieve the pre-baby lifestyle, the banging body or the freedom to shower whenever the fuck you want. Not one person told me *'it's shit at times, you know?'*

I truly believe that if we normalised the conversations around post-partum depression, and I'm not just talking about the day 3 *'baby blues'*, then at least maybe we would stop punishing ourselves for finding it tough.

Yes, I had post-natal depression. Yes, I took anti-depressants, and yes, I went to counselling. Oh, and yes, I've raised a phenomenal little girl, written two books, returned to work and kept all of us alive during the pandemic that I refuse to mention in this book.

It's not easy to take the first step and talk to someone; God, I spoke more about my vagina in the last book than I did about mental health. So I get it. And I know that it's even harder to accept help when your mind is programmed to believe that we have to live up to this fucking *Supermum* pretence that simply does not exist.

If you're reading this now and have felt less than great about life, maybe cried more than you'd like or just don't feel like you anymore, my inbox is open.

Bookmumstheword@hotmail.com

It really is OK to not be OK.

MESS

For fluff's sake, they're messy little sods, aren't they? I feel like I'm living in a post-*Glastonbury Groundhog-day;* strewn drink bottles, empty packets, a pungent yet unidentifiable smell, and the odd worse-for-wear straggler lying on the floor (though this is usually a limbless doll, not an over-excitable *'Gap Yar'* youth). I'm not saying that I don't enjoy a mass clean-up operation every single night of my fucking life, but it'd be nice if, for once, she didn't launch every bloody jigsaw piece onto the floor, or feel the desperate and overwhelming urge to empty her packet of pea-flavoured crisps and dance all over them.

(Oh, Karen, hiya. Yes, I tried *'tidy-up time'* before you suggest it, but Isabelle just looked me square in the face, said *'no Mummy'* and walked off).

I guess I've kind of come to accept my fate, lower my standards and embrace the banana-slime on the wall as her expression of abstract art. It's liberating when you finally acknowledge that your once pristine home is no more, and start celebrating the little wins, like being able to see the carpet at the end of the day, or sitting down without a piece of *Lego* penetrating your arsehole.

I do wonder when she'll learn to tidy up. Hypothetically, I imagined she'd jump right on board with the *'tidy up song'*, but, reflecting on it now, I'd be lucky to see Danny put his own shoes away, never mind a one-year old voluntarily reversing the chaos of the day.

MONEY

Jesus, kids are expensive, aren't they? And not just when they're born either. She seems to be getting pricier all the time. I'd be lying if I said I didn't only take her to the places that were free for under 2s. And I'm sorry but I'm not paying seven quid for her to take a shit in a soft play.

I did actually take her to a soft play a few months ago. Before you think I'm bragging, I wore a dress. A fucking dress. Can you tell that I'm not a regular at these places? I kind of thought that now that she can walk, she would just go and play independently and I'd be able to dead-scroll on my phone whilst scoffing a chocolate muffin in peace. I stupidly thought that the *soft* bit in the title would prevent any major head trauma. Nobody said that I'd be crawling up mammoth, multi-coloured steps with my 2-year old maternity knickers hanging out, all just to rescue my kid from a rope-bridge that she had fallen through and got wedged into. There is genuinely nothing worse than recognising your child's cry at the exact moment that you're about to bite into a blueberry muffin.

And she was too scared to go down the fucking slide that we had spent 15 minutes clambering towards, so we had to crawl back down against the flow of snot-nosed, sweaty toddlers and their miserable, sweaty parents.

You would think that your allocated hour isn't nearly enough time, but trust me, it's plenty.

MUMGOALS

I'm going to have a bit of a rant here (unusual for me, I know). I'm bitterly envious of the mums who have reached a point in their post-partum life where they start the self-care thing again. Look, I'm not bashing self-care, but there is something unifying about spotting another mother with her hair in a greasy bun and a chocolate stain on her jumper. I'm not saying that I don't like the mums in the park with the wet look skinny jeggings, but I just don't think I trust them.

I'm still not loving my post-partum body, and as my child's age moves from weeks to months to years, I'm finding it more difficult to justify the pouch and the fact that I still haven't managed to squeeze my arse back into my jeans. Apparently, there is something called *exercise?* It popped up on my Insta feed once, but I'm convinced it's a scam, so I just ignored it.

N

Nap time

Is there anything more devastating than your child dropping a nap? God, I must have wept for a week. What are you meant to do with them awake for so long? How on earth do you entertain them all day? Isabelle is down to one nap now, and I'm dreading the day that that goes; I didn't sign up for full-day parenting. It sounds bloody horrendous to say that I live for the one hour in the day that she's not with me, but the truth is, some days, I absolutely do.

Some days, I find myself counting down the minutes, wondering when the earliest possible drop time is.

That hour is essential. I do all my life shit in that hour. OK, sometimes I do life shit and sometimes I scroll on Instagram whilst eating *Jaffa Cakes*, but both are equally important to my mental health.

I guess that the day that the final nap goes is the day that I buy her an *iPad*, yeah?

NAPPIES

A year in and I still haven't moved to cloth nappies. I was so conscious of the 200 years it took for every single one of her billions of nappies to biodegrade, and really wanted to make the change, but if I'm honest, I didn't really understand them. Was I meant to scrape the poo out of them? Did I just throw the whole thing into the machine, crap and all? I also didn't fancy the whole load of extra washing when I couldn't even keep up with what we had. (How many days is too many days to wear the same bra? Asking for a friend).

One morning almost tipped me over the edge into *Cloth-bum land*. I crapped myself when I was changing Isabelle (not literally). Her disposable nappy had become so full of wee during the night that it burst, and the silica gel crystals were smeared all over her stomach. I don't know what I thought was in nappies, but I didn't think it was that. In the morning haze, I genuinely thought she'd shat a slush puppy. The sooner she's potty trained the better.

NUMBER TWO

Stop asking women when they're having their babies – whether it is their first or second, or whether they are *chasing a boy* or *trying for a girl.* Please, just stop.

Because secondary infertility.

Because financial worries.

Because relationship strain.

Because post-birth trauma.

Because post-natal depression.

Because the fear of another imperfect maternity leave is real.

Because pregnancy sucked.

Because we're enjoying this one.

Because you don't NEED another child, even if Aunty so-and-so says it's unfair to just have the one. Yes, the transition to toddlerdom was tinged with sadness, as the teeny newborn (the main contributor to my semi-breakdown in the first book) slipped away from my grasp and was replaced with an increasingly independent toddler.

I'd be lying if I didn't acknowledge the shed tear as I packed up her discarded sensory toys, over-snug babygrows and cellular blankets, to be replaced with Lego, big girl pyjamas and the cutest little duvet I'd ever seen.

So, for a moment, I grieved being Mum to a baby; my burnt-out mind reminiscing fictional coffee mornings with friends and the ease of a breastfeed over the need to provide actual food three times a day.

When my closest mum friends announced their second pregnancies, I found myself questioning whether I wanted another; the suitability of the age gap, the cost of two children in nursery, whether we could fit a double buggy in the boot.

I know that I had always imagined having two children. But honestly, that was before I'd had one. It's hard, ok? The struggle to juggle life and money and time and remembering who the fuck you are only just started falling into place for me when Isabelle was around 18 months old. But, alongside the conundrums of practicality and finances, I feared that another baby would ruin my marriage.

Everyone knows that falling madly in love with someone else would push your relationship to the brink, but nobody told me that the 'someone else' could be your own child. I changed immeasurably when I became a mother; not only my physical appearance – mum-bun and mum-tum - but my mind. I couldn't switch off. I felt, and still feel, as though I'm in hyper-aware mode; constantly cleaning, planning and making sure she doesn't fucking kill herself. It's beyond exhausting, but I just don't know how to switch it off. So, I guess that when she's asleep, and I finally have some time for myself again, I just want to power down: no talking, no touching and certainly no rumpy-pumpy.

Without the rumpy-pumpy it's pretty difficult to conceive a child, even if I was ready for one, but, more truthfully, I wasn't sure Danny or I would make it out alive if we had another just yet. It had taken us a year and a half to finally feel like we weren't drowning, so I'm really not too sure whether I want to throw the apple cart off the side of a cliff once again (as the saying goes).

So, here's a bit of advice from the woman who hates people who give advice, stop telling me that *'Isabelle needs a little brother or sister',* unless you're planning on breeding and rearing them yourself. I'm not ready.

NURSERY

Nursery is pretty cool, to be fair. Isabelle has come on SO much since she started going in June 2020. She absolutely loves her key workers, and they genuinely adore her. Yes, it costs more than an all-inclusive week in the Maldives, but can you put a price on your child's development? (Answer: yes. £51 a day, and rising each September).

AND, in addition to the eye-watering, sky-high prices, I've had a tip-off that SOME parents are also smuggling in treats for the staff. I got speaking to the leader of the Baby Room, who told me that some sneaky-ass mums are pushing contraband in through their kid's bag, every single Friday for the key workers. Now, I'm all for thanking the staff, but what is their motive for this? I reckon it's a pushy mum's attempt to bribe the girls, so that their kid gets an extra 10 minutes with the flash cards. It's not on, and whilst I'm appalled by their manipulative behaviour, I'm half-tempted to see if a box of cookies will be enough to persuade them to lay off the messy play; I've been finding bits of congealed pasta in her hair for weeks.

Of course, the tight-arse in me ensures that she is there from the moment the doors open until the final minute (but definitely before those additional charges – a fiver for every five minutes after half six?! So I'll see you at 18.29, shall I?) and I swear I've absolutely, definitely, one hundred percent not sat in the car until the final minute just to maximise my headspace (and insta-scrolling).

I've still not quite mastered the pick-up etiquette. Yes, I know you say the kids name and they go and get her (and only once have they brought the wrong kid out) but I still don't know how you do the *'Nursery Mum friend'* thing. For example, Isabelle has come home today banging on about a kid called

Harry. Apparently, he is her little best mate in nursery and they do everything together. But it's odd if I linger round waiting to find out who Harry and his Mum are, isn't it? (Though when Danny found out that she had a *'boyfriend',* he was more than ready to pay Harry a personal visit, *Den of Thieves* style).

Anyway, I'd take a pick-up over a drop-off any day, particularly in the early days: Isabelle would unexpectedly decide to completely lose her shit just as we got to the door, point-blank refusing to enter the building. The poor apprentice nursery nurse had to drag her in kicking and screaming. Bet that's put her off kids for life.

And though I moan about the price, they do give her some fancy food. I'm sure during my nursery days we were given toast, milk and a bourbon. Nowadays, they're on duck a l'orange and chicken jambalaya, with fancy starters like a cheese and chive muffin or pitta bread and hummus. Apparently, she eats all of it too, despite only eating half of her meals at home (and that's mainly the chips). But, even though we're old and mature enough to rear a child (so they say), we as parents aren't yet brave enough to actually ask the staff what the portion sizes are like at nursery, so we just surreptitiously search for food on the pictures uploaded to the *Parentzone* app, to get a vague idea as to how much she's actually eaten.

I feel like nursery inductions should come with a three-day course on nursery etiquette, actually. Like, I didn't know the rules around fundraising, either. When Isabelle came home with a sponsor form (on her first fucking day, I might add) to raise money via a *'sponsored virtual walk'* to Chester Zoo, Dan and I went into panic mode. You see, we didn't want to look like the tight-arse family, so we asked everyone we knew to sponsor her (though I'm still not convinced that a bunch of under 3s walked anywhere, never mind 26 virtual miles to Chester fucking Zoo).

Anyway, on the big day, we sent Isabelle into nursery dressed as a giraffe with an envelope full of sponsor money, and two sheets of A4 brimming with sponsors. The nursery <u>as a whole</u> raised just short of £500, a fifth of which was raised by our family alone. We looked like animal-loving, cash-shifting ballers. And I don't even like the zoo.

I do have to laugh at some of the outfits she comes home in, though. Despite me folding everything from tops to socks into a neat, fool-proof bundle (well, for the first month, at least) she often comes home dressed like a curious, part-time closet cross-dresser – a belly-hugging string vest on top and a tutu with leggings on the bottom. We've nicknamed *nursery Isabelle* as *'Dave from Hull'.* Occasionally, she even upgrades her outfit midway through the day, like she's had a private rendezvous with Gok Wan in the sandpit. She's sent in dressed head to toe in *Primark* and waltzes out in someone else's *Zara* coat or *Joules* leggings (I bet these belong to the kid whose mother sneaks in fucking biscuits; who in their right mind sends their kid into nursery in fancy-schmancy clothes? I don't even stretch to *Joules* for a family wedding). Obviously, her dad doesn't notice that she's dressed entirely in someone else's clobber, but I'm not 100% convinced that he would notice if he collected the wrong kid, if I'm completely honest.

But best thing of all about nursery? She's knackered when she gets home. Straight to bed, sweetie. Night night.

NURTURING

The second year is when they start to truly develop their gorgeous, if not ever-so-slightly sassy, little personalities. Their individuality shines through, and their interests become apparent. Isabelle (somehow) has a very loving and nurturing side. She loves nothing more than caring for her babies; hushing them to sleep and kissing their heads goodnight. Of course, I find this just beautiful to witness; it even prompted me to contemplate her role as a big sister for the first time. But, within minutes, as if she'd had a message from the womb, or a flashback to her mother crying herself to sleep 12 months ago, she launched the doll head-first onto the floor, shouted *'uh-oh'* and ran off. Thanks Isabelle, for smacking me right back down to reality.

Her impromptu violent streak may have something to do with her well-meaning parents, who, after witnessing Isabelle stuffing a veggie puff into the mouth of her dolly, attempted to remove the occlusion by giving back blows (I know it's only a doll, but I didn't want a rotten crisp breeding inside her, and my job as a dysphagia – broken swallow-specialist left me uneasy at the thought of an albeit hypothetical airway occlusion).

Luckily, the blockage was dislodged and the dolly made a full recovery, even if she now frequently falls victim to a teeny do-gooder, smacking her on the back after every mouthful.

Of course, her love for dollies means that, once again, my living room is full of baby shit: bottles, nappies, a teeny little bath, a cot, pram and dummies galore. All for her fucking doll. It's as if we're a family of four; the plastic kid does everything with us. I have to bath her, change her bum and I've even had to start sticking her shit paintings on the fridge, too.

O

Oops

I accidentally volleyed Isabelle whilst trying to replicate the *Hey Duggee* dance today. Oops.

I'd like to tell you that accidents are few and far between, but anyone who has ever met a toddler will know that they attract danger like flies to shit.

Take last Monday, for example. I'll set the scene; 19 month old Isabellend is becoming increasingly independent and demanding to dress herself. Hoorah! One job less for me. Or it would be if she didn't have the tenacity of a sloth and the manual dexterity of a pissed-up octopus. She wanted to put her tights on. I helped with the feet, and her job was simply to pull them up. That's it. Yet, within seconds, she gave up and started penguin-waddling away, her legs bound together. I politely asked her to return, which, of course, she completely ignored, and made her waddling-way to the door. Pre-empting disaster, I rose to my feet to collect her, but of course, she mistook that as the start of a game of 'chase the half-dressed toddler' and broke into a run, tripping head-first into the door frame. I promise I didn't say 'that's your own fucking fault' under my breath.

At least I've stopped smashing her skull on the way out of the car seat now. Instead, I place her on the floor, and, almost daily, she walks into the open car door, whacking her head on that perfectly-positioned spikey bit on the underside. Again, I'm putting it down as character building, or sheer life incompetence through which I take no blame.

One absolute mumfail that I can't blame her for is the time that I tried to shut the dining room door whilst her fingers were wedged between the door and the frame – Officer, it wasn't intentional, honestly. Completely oblivious to her trapped hand, I kept pulling on the door, against the resistance caused by my daughter's own bones. She was so pained by my incompetence as a mother that she did that silent scream cry, reserved only for the most excruciating of injuries. I should note that no toddlers were seriously physically harmed in this incident, though I can't yet comment on the long-term psychological effects of her mortified mother repeatedly jamming her fingers in a doorframe.

Organised

Motherhood requires a whole other level of organisation. I thought I was an organised person in school, with my array of gel pens and post-it note varieties. Oh, what I wouldn't give to go back to that child now and say *'girl, you have no idea'.*

That young girl had no clue that meal-prep was even a thing: to actually pick what you want to eat weeks in advance, and make it in batches, to save your future-self time, money and your arse when you get the sick-inducing realisation that *'fuck, it's five o'clock and I've not fed her'.* It's marvellous when it's done, but it's an absolute bitch to do. I either have all the ingredients in, and no time (or motivation), or find myself with a spare half-an-hour during an unexpectedly long nap, and I'm all out of veg.

Of course, when I do meal prep, I'm like Mrs Trunchball's *'Cookie'*; a sweaty, snot-covered mess with greasy hair and an inability to control the portion sizes. Subsequently, I run out of tupperware every single time. Cue me loading up anything with a lid to store a week's worth of shepherd's pie in the freezer. I think last week I even used the box that her bath toys came in.

You've also got to be ahead of the game for nursery, too. Each month, they send out a date list for special activities that they have planned, such *as 'Scotland Day', 'Wear Red Wednesday' or 'we-haven't-fucked-over-the-mums-enough Monday'.* It's a shitting nightmare. I completely missed her Christmas party alert, sending her in in a paint-stained pair of jeans to meet the Big Man: the only non-festive child in the whole nursery.

She's only in two days a week, and I pray each month that the bastard events list only features dates on a Tuesday, Thursday and Friday.

P

PARENTING STYLES

Last year, parenting styles weren't really an issue. Danny and I were both pretty much in agreement that we needed to feed and clothe her, and that we wanted her to sleep as much as possible, particularly during the night. Simple.

This year, when behaviour and discipline came into play, we had to start discussing parenting styles. And that's when the *fun* began. Do you shout or patiently explain? Do you let the child lead or do you take control? Do you let them engage in risky play, or do you protect them from harm at all costs? Who knows (nobody on Google, that's for sure). My aim is to instil some sort of authority and respect whilst also letting her explore the world in a safe and loving environment. If anyone has cracked that, then please hit me up, because, as it happens, the requirement to figure out how the fuck to parent a child has caused some conflict between Danny and I. It's not that either of us are wrong, but, well, he's not right, put it that way.

This is in no way a public apology to Danny, but I've noticed that my standards vary depending on who is instilling the authority. When Daddy is leading, I'll get so mad at him if he loses his temper with her; my beautiful, sweet and innocent little angel. But when she ignores her mama, I will royally lose my shit.

It's probably only just hit me that this parenting lark lasts longer than the baby and toddler stage, too.

We're on this whole decision-making, *'don't fuck her up'* journey now until we, or she, dies. Bleak.

I want to be the mum who has read all the books and understands the process of child development; that her behaviour is her way of exploring the world and its boundaries, within the safety of her family unit. I want to have the patience of a saint, and the time to listen and celebrate every thought and emotion that she experiences. But, I also want to be able to get my weekly shop done in under an hour, and defecate without a toddler's instalment of *Question Time.* Oh, what I wouldn't give for a solitary shit.

I often wonder how many decisions a parent has to make in their lifetime? How one wrong decision could royally fuck the whole path up entirely. I know that I should trust my instincts, but what do you do if even they are arguing with one another? One is shouting at me to *'do flashcards in Spanish'* and the other is telling me that I could probably go back to bed if I set her up with enough snacks and a Youtube two-hour special of *Peppa Pig* (or *Cerdo Peppa,* for the angry, Spanish-obsessed woman in my head).

PARK LIFE

Not the crazy festival in Manchester, or the 90s hit by *Blur*, but the reality of parenting a toddler: a damp bench, screaming children, a parking lot of prams and scooters, and a rogue child whose parents have no fucks left to give. This child usually attaches themselves to you, wanting you to pick them up and talk to them about their friends or their day in school, or that their *'little brother is called Barney and he is two and he likes ice cream',* as if I give a rat's arse. I'm only there myself to tire my daughter out, I don't want to talk and I certainly don't want to adopt another snot-nosed kid. I envy the

mother who can ignore their child for 20 minutes –
mine is too small to explore independently, because
the council have helpfully made the mini climbing
frame toddler-friendly, apart from that fucking
ridiculous metal bit with the huge holes in, that she
would inevitably fall to her death from if she were
alone.

Though she can climb the steps to the slide
independently, she will ultimately freak out at the
top and either attempt to jump off, or go down the
slide head first, and whilst it'd be hilarious to watch,
I haven't got the time or the patience to sit in A&E.
My friend shared her fear of her daughter's shoes
sticking on the slide and her toppling face-first over
the side, so now I can't get that image out of my head
and hate every second we're there, unless she's
securely strapped into a swing and can't move from
my sight. Even then, the joy is dissipated by the
burning retinas of the queuing families behind you,
impatiently waiting for their turn. How long is a

decent turn on a swing? I feel like there should be some guidance on swing etiquette for us newbies, or one of those sand timers that they have in a sauna (remember saunas?).

Oh, and then there are those weird massive swings (*Yakka Dee* said that these are called *basket swings* – every day's a school day) that you can just lie the kid in and push, but they're only really useful for kids who don't move, unlike mine.

Making the decision to leave the park is usually triggered by an accident or a tantrum, both of which are avoidable if you just don't go to the park in the first place. The only way out is by enforcing snack-related bribery tactics, which ruin their appetite for lunch. The trip always ends with a highly-emotional and over-tired child, who sleeps in the car on the way home. Of course, they will wake up as soon as you arrive back at the house, still knackered but with enough energy to fervently refuse a proper nap; which was the only fucking reason you took them there in the first place.

PATIENCE

Patience isn't a virtue, it's a fucking essential criterion on the job spec for a mother, alongside minimal expectations for self-care, hygiene and sleep. So, if you're venturing into a career in Toddlerdom, here are some top tips for interview prep:

- Nothing will ever test your patience more than a half-naked child on the landing. You can prep for this by shouting aimlessly into the abyss.
- Toddlers walk SO fucking slowly. I know your legs are small, but we've walked 20 metres in

half an hour. Prep for this by pacing forward and back over 3ft of ground, for an hour a day.

- The length of time taken to prepare a meal is indirectly correlated to the number of seconds it takes for the child to launch it on the floor, accompanied by a satanic laugh and a demand for *'choc-choc'*. Prep for this by spending 45 minutes slaving over a hot stove in the kitchen, then just smear the dinner up the wall.

- Every reachable surface will be smeared in sticky fingerprints within hours of a mammoth house-clean (what's the fucking point?). Prep for this by raking leaves with a kitchen fork, in a hurricane.

- Your tolerance towards your husband's inability to put the dishes in the dishwasher, rather than next to the fucking dishwater, will wear thin, and you will want to smack him in the face with a pan. Prep for this with deep breathing exercises, or just hide all of the pans (just in case).

- Standing on a wooden block or one of those jigsaw piece with the bastard peg-handle thing on will make you want to scream. Know that you can't scream, because the kid will then cry and steal your thunder. Prep for this by jumping bare-foot on an upturned plug socket.

- You will notice that other, childless women can treat themselves to nice, new things, like clothes, or make-up, or lip fillers. The only trout pout you'll be getting is when your child accidentally nuts you. And remember, no matter how much that head-butt hurts, your tears aren't worth their attention-seeking, retaliation tantrum. Prep for this by head-butting the corner of a brick wall.

- Remember that husband I told you about before? He also tends to put a pile of clean washing back into the dirty washing pile, just for shits and giggles. It makes me want to smother him with a freshly-laundered pillow. Prep for this by googling *'chokehold'* (I'm kidding, of course. A knee in the nuts is more effective).

PETS

Remember being a child and desperately wanting a pet?

Well, Daddy thinks that our one-year old is already at that stage, so when she, at 13 months, said *'fis'*, he was convinced that she was *asking* for a pet fish. The following day, I came home to three additional mouths to feed and the smell of a urine infection in my kitchen. Three nameless goldfish had made their home on my breakfast bar (as they couldn't actually be left within reach of the one-year old they were bought for, lest her eat them whole for a midday snack).

Obviously, two of them died within a week because Mummy refused to feed them and Daddy's excitement wore off pretty quickly. That was until he took pity on the lonely fish and bought it four friends. FML.

Now, Isabelle asks to feed them and enjoys dropping their fish food into the tank, often sampling it first. I was mortified, but as it turns out, it contains seafood, vitamins and minerals, which, if I'm honest, is probably healthier than the majority of food I make for her.

PHONES

I'm embarrassed to say that I'm probably addicted to social media.

I'm adamant that I don't want her to see me staring into my phone, but I'm not strong-willed enough to actually leave it alone for longer than 20 minutes, so I'll either try, and fail, to stealth use it just out of her eyeline, or I'll hide in the kitchen to aimlessly check my messages in the hunt for a dopamine hit, as if the perfect, most hilariously-wonderful little shot of happiness wasn't running around my living room.

I know that if we can't strike a balance to maintain a real-world presence, we are ultimately at risk of missing out on the beautiful nuances of child development that are happening right in front of us: the way they now copy a dance move or imitate your speech, the way they seek eye contact for reassurance, or make their dolly *'drink'* some juice. But, I'd be lying if I said the battle with the black mirror wasn't constant. I am trying to always be present and engaged with Isabelle first, but it's not easy.

We are the first generation to bring up children immersed in an online world. We *Google* answers to life's biggest questions and crave a numerical rating in the form of *'likes'* for every picture of our #familydayout.

I wish that we could go back to a simpler time. One in which I didn't have to use social media to promote my books; a world where we weren't rated by follower count and story content, but the sad truth is that we absolutely are. I can't change it, and because all I have ever wanted to do is to make her proud, I'll have to add the phone juggle to my list of increasing mum guilt moments.

POO

It needs to be mentioned, because, well, when do mums stop talking about poo? Is it weird to say that I'd trade in these fully-solid nuclear nuggets for the vinegar shits any day? There is something slightly vile about changing a fully-formed, grown-up poo, and yet, shit on my hands doesn't even phase me anymore, and I'm not sure whether that's successful parenting, or just the saddest thing I've ever heard.

POTTY TRAINING

Now, this book documents the second year of parenting, and if you're at this stage now and thinking, *'what the fuck, I haven't potty trained yet'*, don't worry, neither have I.

I have, however, started exploring the potty with her (sometimes more intently than I'd like). She's starting to tell me that she needs a poo, and I want to start the conversations in a view to *'getting her ready'.* Because that's the thing, isn't it? Everyone says *'wait until they're ready'* as if one day they're going to say to you, *'Mum, I want to stop defecating in my pants now, do you have a receptacle I can put this faeces in?'.*

I have no idea how to start all that, but I have come up with an ingenious idea to get the ball rolling. OK, hear me out. Isabelle loves *Hey Duggee*, so I've convinced her that the way to get *Duggee* to play on the TV is by sitting on the potty. That's right, the TV is controlled by her arse; she sits down, the TV comes on, she stands up, it goes off. Magic. She's bloody into it as well; she will sit there for ages!

Of course, there are flaws to my plan, like what happens when there isn't a TV there, or why she can't sit there all day. But I'll figure that bit out. For now, I'm just impressed with the operant conditioning of my child, like Skinner's rats, or Danny's sex life.

Pressure

It took me months to finally realise, and accept, that, as a mother, the buck stops with me. That, no matter how arsed, or not arsed, I feel, it is me who has to meal plan, it's me who has to wash her hair, and get her to nursery in whatever themed fancy dress it is this week, with her sponsor money and (shop-bought) baked goods (I'm not fucking superwoman).

You're never off duty and the responsibility is infinite, and relentless. It's pretty damn terrifying.

Like, those fingernails; they grow so fucking fast. The week flies around, and, before I know it, it's the night before nursery again and I'm fighting with her to clip off her talons before she claws the face off a toddler. Because nobody else will do it. No-one. Danny is bloody brilliant, but he's blind to the nuances of parenting: the empty nappy sack packet, the low-running snacks or the piss-wet wellies that render them useless. Yesterday, he asked me why we don't have a spare winter coat that fits Isabelle. Answer: Because I haven't fucking bought one yet. Because, for one second, my mind slipped right through the piles of washing, over the dirty playroom floor and past the over-flowing cardboard bin. It just slipped out of my head, and nobody else bought one. It's mad that, isn't it? If I don't do it, it just doesn't get done.

The responsibility of a whole human is in my hands. And as she grows from a baby to a toddler, the responsibility grows, too. OK, so I'm not keeping her alive with my tits alone anymore, but I still have to find food for her. Every bloody day. In fact, I think that's harder. At least I didn't have to think about the unsaturated fat content of breastmilk. All her veg was wrapped up in a beautiful, if only slightly veiny, nipple-sealed package. And now? It is considered a *good week* if she hasn't had a takeaway and the fruit she's eating didn't have to have the mould scraped off it (why does fruit go mouldy so quickly? You don't get that with biscuits).

What's more, we have to shape and define these little people. We have to turn them into beautiful, independent and strong humans, who aren't dicks or psychopaths or Tories. We have to educate them, teach them right from wrong, a sense of humour, kindness, love and compassion. How much pressure is that?

I've started consciously avoiding parenting books. For a bit, I sought guidance in the ultimate mission, but it seems like you can't not fuck it up in one way or another: don't let them cry and they'll be needy forever, let them cry and they'll have huge attachment issues. Discipline them so they know right from wrong, but don't shout – it'll emotionally scar them for life.

The truth is, I don't have a clue what the answer is. If you do, message me, or more preferably, tell me that you don't know, either. There is unity in a consensus of cluelessness.

Pretend play

I actually really love this bit. The first time she fed me a mouthful of pretend soup from a toy spatula I could have cried. It was a moment to treasure, even if she did ram it into the back of my throat. The novelty does wear off after around 25 minutes of eating non-existent soup from an undoubtedly contaminated communal spoon, but still, it's precious for a bit.

At our first *'parents' evening'* at nursery (how bloody cute is that, by the way?) her key worker said that Isabelle loved role play; and they're always finding her in the little home corner, comforting dollies and putting them to bed. Though my heart fluttered as I imagined her *'being Mummy',* a wave of nausea overcame me at the thought of her re-enacting our bedtime routine. I wonder whether she pins down the dollies to brush their teeth, and mutters *'for fuck's sake, Isabelle'* under her breath, as the dolly refuses the final nappy change of the day.

It is fascinating watching these teeny little people try to replicate what they see around the house, though I would like to put out a written request to the *Early Learning Centre:* if you're going to make kids' hoovers, make it so that they work, hey?

PULL-UPS

Moving away from traditional nappies to pull-ups once again highlighted how little we are taught about how the fuck to dress a child. After purchasing the *'big-girl'* nappies, I was excited to try Isabelle in them straight away. Putting them on is like them wearing a pair of knickers, and often involves a bare arse sitting on your crossed legs as you feed their feet into the holes, and then pull them up before the kid pisses in your lap. Fine. What I hadn't figured out was how to take them off. The first time Isabelle shat in her pull-ups, I didn't yet know about the side-rip technique, so pulled them down like underpants. Cue the nappy folding inside out and a shit falling out onto the living room floor. Please tell me I'm not the only moron who's done this? Note to Pampers: can you just write *rip the side* on the packaging, please?

PYJAMAS

Replacing babygrows with pyjamas hurts like a kick in the tit. Suddenly, your precious infant has poofed into thin air, and you've found yourself putting an actual child to bed. Of course, it's easier to change the arse of a toddler, without those bastard poppers, but I miss the tired lolling of a sleepy-headed baby wandering around my house.

Q

QUIET

Silence isn't golden. It's a sign that something destructive is happening just out of sight. You must go and investigate immediately. Be prepared to find:

- a colossal spillage, usually of something ridiculously difficult to get out of the carpet, like talc, or *Nutella*, or, on one occasion, *Dulux* emulsion

- an imminent disaster involving a child wielding a sharp implement (how the fuck did she get hold of a bread knife?)

- Bozo the clown, deep in your make up bag, with a £17.50 *MAC* lipstick smushed between their teeth, and your brand new bronzer smashed to pieces in their lap

- a studious little girl practicing phonics independently in her bedroom

(the last one is a myth)

R

RAISINS

They're obsessed with them. I don't give parenting advice, but I will tell you this: raisins are life. Take. Them. Everywhere.

Just don't look at the sugar content. Repeat to self *'it's dried fruit, it's just dried fruit'.*

READING

Before you freak out and call me Karen, no, she can't read yet. But, I am a massive advocate for bedtime stories and love sharing books with her. I always imagined that special moment; snuggled up with her on the couch, reading her favourite book as she happily pointed to the pictures and giggled along with the story. Aww.

I definitely didn't imagine the reality; Isabelle thrusting a book in my face, then, within seconds of me reading the first few pages, shouting *'no'* and removing the book from my hands only to replace it with another; the cycle continuing until I lose my shit.

If ever she does get comfy and listen to the story, she will turn the pages well before I'm ready, and, well, it just ruins the flow of the story doesn't it?

And don't get me started on sound books. WHO thought it would be a good idea to buy <u>the full collection</u> of the interactive music books from *Aldi,* that play the bastard nursery rhyme on repeat (with no off switch, I might add). The words in the book are just the lyrics of the nursery rhyme, which no human could sing and turn as quickly as the song is played, nor would ever read as an actual book. What a con. Of course, she loves these the most and happily presses the button over 35 times a day. Yay.

REPETITION

I'm beyond a broken record now, I'm a broken woman. I'm not sure how many times I have to repeat myself repeat myself repeat myself, but if someone gave me a pound each time, I can tell you now, I'd be sipping some fancy-schmancy cocktail called *'Mother's meltdown'* or *'Alaskya Dad'* on a private island, alone.

I mean, HOW many times do I have to say:

- *What's in your mouth?*
- *Get down*
- *Spit it out*
- *No Isabelle*
- *Come here and put your nappy on*
- *Where's your shoes?*
- *Daddy's on the toilet (again)*
- *Up the stairs please*
- *It's bedtime now*

Of course, her response to these is to continue banging the baby gate against the wall and staring aimlessly into space, pretending that she hasn't heard a word (just like her father).

S

SELF-CARE

When did shitting in peace become self-care? As much as I love this kid, her standing over me as I poo, giving a running commentary like it's a spectator sport, just isn't appreciated. Daddy, on the other hand, gets a 45-minute shit with full wi-fi access, a fully-functioning lockable door and the option of either crisps or a chocolate bar. I'm sure he's just hiding in there until she's ready for Uni.

Just the idea of self-care excites me, but the guilt associated with doing something I love, rather than cleaning the kitchen or folding that mound of washing, isn't worth carrying.

I can't remember the last time I moisturised. I don't know when I last wore a non-covid-related face mask, and I certainly can't recall the last time I gave myself a pedicure, beyond dry-cutting my toenails over a bin, because they've started catching in my sock or slicing open a neighbouring toe.

God, I have to rely on a cartoon pork just to clean my own vagina. (I should explain, I mean *Peppa* on the TV distracting her whilst I wash, I don't actually use a gammon loofer). My self-care stretches to clicking on a sponsored post on Facebook, for a moustache trimmer.

I know I need to find time for me, but after a day of giving all the love I've got, I haven't got the energy to find more.

SHARING

You may be thinking, *'Wow, a one-year old is sharing! What a great skill! She's so advanced!'*

Nah, she couldn't give a flying rat's arse about sharing her toys. In fact, she will smack any child who comes close to even touching her stuff, even if she didn't care for it less than half a second ago.

What she will share is her food. Specifically, her half-eaten, moistened crisps or soggy, partially-chewed banana. She's determined, too; she will forcefully ram it into your mouth and watch intently to make sure you chew and swallow. This repeats until you vomit, or she runs out of snacks. How lovely.

What is worse than this is her expectation that I will share my food. And, for the *Friends* fans, Joey and I are very similar in our stance on food-sharing. Particularly when it comes to *'choc-choc'*. *Hypothetical Mum-me* would argue that I wouldn't share chocolate on the basis of it being extremely unhealthy for my innocent and unspoilt daughter, but in reality, I just don't want to share my damn *Dairy Milk*. It's my one vice. I love her, I do, I just don't love her enough to give her *my last Rolo*. So, I've taken to hiding in the kitchen to stealth scoff *Quality Street* while she's destroying the living room. You've got to pick your battles.

SHOES

Around the age of one, kids learn to walk. Now, I whooped and hollered with the rest of them when she took her first steps, it was a glorious moment and I truly was beaming with joy from almost every orifice. The problem is, when they've learnt, they can't unlearn. And the novelty wears off very quickly when their ability to walk comes with a point-blank refusal to ever sit in their pram again. Why *would* you sit in a pram when you can walk (albeit at the pace of a dying sloth)? Cue me walking at 20 yards an hour for the next year.

Anyway, guidance suggests that you need to keep kids barefoot for as long as possible, to help the development of their teeny little feet. Again, this comes with the small hinderance of the rest of the world giving no shits; glass, stones and Lego are scattered everywhere, just ready to slice open their little soles within minutes, and that's just in my living room. So off to *Clarks* we went (and by we, I mean Danny and his Mum. I can't stand the place and £36 for a pair of ugly shoes that fit for all of 3 days makes me want to vomit). At the ripe old age of 11 months, Isabelle was a size 4G in shoes (I remember because I'm a wonderful mother, nothing to do with phone data). It's a useless piece of information though, as no other shops have the G bit, so you either need to re-mortgage your house or sell your spleen and commit to shopping in *Clarks*, or you just ignore the G and hope their feet don't get mutilated by *George's* finest.

SMELL

Remember that newborn baby smell? The irresistible olfactogasm of a freshly cooked human; all warm and snuggly and perfect? Well that's gone. She stinks. Not all the time, I do wash her (mainly when we have visitors or if she's off to nursery because Danny has a complex about her being the smelly kid of the class). But her feet smell now. How do I know? Because she thinks it's hilarious to smell them, and the feet of unsuspecting visitors, and shout *'POOOO'*. And her head smells like *sweaty head*. And, though she's yet to get whiffy pits, I'm still grieving my stench-free bubba.

SNACKS

If there's a key to heaven, it's shaped like a snack. Want the kid to sit in their car seat? Snack. Want them to just stay still for two bastard minutes whilst you change a particularly vulgar nappy? Snack. Want to prevent them climbing out of a trolley mid big shop? Snack snack snack, snack snack snack. I surrendered today to the ultimate mum-bribe; opening a pack of blueberries, THAT I HADN'T YET PAID FOR, in *ASDA*. Wow, I felt like a rebel. We were never allowed to do that as a kid, and here I was, bending the rules in my local supermarket, just to keep Satan at bay. It turns out that 89p is a reasonable price to pay to prevent the glares of the entire fruit aisle as you karate chop a stiff-as-a-board one-year old into a trolley seat. I'm not going to lie though, I did ensure that every shopper was aware of my commitment to paying for the goods; elaborately waving the empty packet around before placing it on the conveyor belt.

I must add, I'm not a healthy Helen. Please don't assume that fruit is my number one go to. Of course, I'd like it to be, but let's be honest, nobody wants to find a mouldy strawberry wedged down the side of a car seat. For months, I thought I was smashing motherhood by giving her those oaty bars; she loved them and I relished in the fact that they were as healthy as could be. That was until I realised that they had more sugar in them than a *Freddo*. No wonder she was bouncing off the fucking walls. Oops.

Being a toddler's snack bitch is, dare I say it, more exhausting than being their dairy cow. I know that she can eat snacks independently now, but at least I always had milk on tap. Now, Mother of God help me if I don't have a variety of tasty treats on hand at all times. Of course, I could instil discipline and self-control, but I have no idea how to do that, so I'll remain a walking, talking tuck box for as long as it keeps her quiet.

Speech and language

Wow, how fascinating is language development? I know that I'm a Speech and Language Therapist, so watching her communication develop was always going to activate my inner-geek, but it's truly incredible witnessing a relatively useless baby morph into a fully-fledged miniature chatterbox.

It was just gorgeous hearing her say '*Mummy*' for the first time, especially if it was accompanied by a cuddle or the offer of a half-eaten crisp that she'd saved just for me.

Those early days used to fill me with pride as she hollered '*hiya*' at every passer-by in *ASDA*, even if I did have to bite my tongue at the misery arses who didn't return her greeting. The first time I asked her to shut the fridge door and she did it, I was ready to call *MENSA;* though I quickly hung up when she pointed at my tea, shouted '*hot*' and then fisted it anyway.

Everything was just wonderful, until the '*no*' came along. It crept up on me out of nowhere; like a bear in the woods, or a car insurance renewal date. All of a sudden, my gorgeous baby girl answered every question with a sassy, head-shaking and 100% confident '*no*':

'*Please can you put your coat on?*'

'No'

'Shall we go to bed now?'

'No'

'Please stop standing on dolly's head'

'No'.

I've started asking her double negatives to throw her off the scent and finally get shit done.

Despite her dictator-like refusal to cooperate with any of my reasonable requests, I do enjoy the hilarity that comes with the *copying phase*. She repeats the last word in every sentence we say, like that irritating parrot on *Peppa Pig*. I'd be lying if I said I didn't cry the first time she said *'love you'*, even if she simply echoed it back to me with no comprehension of meaning.

Obviously, her new fascination with repetition has meant that I need to watch my potty-mouth, which I enforce by telling her *stickhead* dad to *go fluff himself*.

But before you empathise with him, hear me out. I'm furious because Isabelle has started calling me *'Bec'*, as he never remembers, or rather, chooses not, to call me *'Mummy'*. I don't get what his issue is, it's hardly as creepy as me calling him *'Daddy'*, like we're in some kind of submissive, naughty school-girl role play. Just the thought makes my skin-crawl (as you can tell, my post-child libido is yet to make an appearance).

Regardless of our effort to avoid expletives, her language acquisition has still resulted in some unintentional corkers. For months, Isabelle would say *'piss'* for please, which didn't always go down well with the blue rinse brigade in *Marks & Spencer's* café.

Walking the cold streets in December, Isabelle would shout *'Christmas Shites'* whilst pointing at the festive decorations (I agree that they were a bit tacky, but *shite* seemed rude, particularly as the home owner was within ear shot).

But my favourite articulatory faux pas has to be *'dipshit';* her variant of *lipstick*. It's brilliant, even if it did result in an awkward apology to a chav who was sampling *Collection 2000* at a *Boots* make-up counter.

Anyway, I digress. At 17 months, Isabelle started saying *'why'.* Now I know I sound like a Susan boasting about my highly-advanced child, but that couldn't be further from the truth. I don't know if you've ever explained why you have to go to bed to a one-year old, but no answer is satisfactory for them. She stood at her baby gate for 20 minutes shouting *'WHY, MUMMY? WHYYYYYYYY?'* like 90s throwback *Kenan* having a meltdown (google it, Millennials).

And yet, within all of these speechy escapades, I find nothing more exasperating than when that chatterbox child clams up completely whenever you actually want to show off their linguistic ability to another human. It's as if every word she'd ever heard fell immediately out of her head as soon as the poised listener walked into the room. Instead, she sits in silence, staring blankly at you as you demand animal noises from her, like a dick.

Subsequently, you'll feel like a back-street car salesman trying to flog a write-off, as you *'swear she was doing it five minutes ago'*. The whole playdate is then spent desperately trying to get them to produce any kind of verbal output, in a last-ditch attempt to prove that they do actually know the sound a horse makes, even though the visitor couldn't give two shits, and probably can't understand a word that your child is saying anyway.

Standards

Your standards will slip. You'll start accepting a shower every other day, and dry shampoo will be a weekly essential, not just a bit of slobbery that you embrace on day three of a festival. You won't hesitate to wipe a snotty nose with your sleeve, and then continue to wear that jumper for the next day or   so.

Your idea of *living your best life* will be shit-free fingernails and a new episode of *Hey Duggee.*

You will initially send your child into nursery in beautifully-ironed, perfectly-matching clothes. That will last less than a month. *'Just fucking get dressed and let's go'* will be a frequent morning chant, and you'll be proud if you only swear under your breath that day. Success will be based on whether your child has a pair of matching shoes on. You will cease to care about matching socks, and you'll use up the ill-fitting nappies, even when they've gone a size up, because *'you've got ten left and you're not wasting them'.*

You'll eat pre-chewed leftovers for dinner on some nights, because you can't be arsed cooking for yourself, and the toaster is *'all the way in the kitchen'.*

STICKS

What is it with sticks? They love them! I can't even recall ever talking to her about *sticks,* and yet, she's somehow lovingly adopted and invited home a full family of them to ~~rot~~ live with us.

I guess sticks are the original imaginative play prop. With a little creativity, a stick becomes: a wand, a sword, a pen, a stirring spoon, a poker, a walking aid or a broom (or, of course, a phallus, if you hold the maturity of a shrew, like my husband).

What I didn't quite envisage was that my parental duties would extend beyond my daughter, to incorporate my newly adopted sticks. Yesterday, I had to bathe, feed and clothe them, after rescuing them from the path on our morning walk. What a high point in my life.

T

TANTRUMS

Bloody toddlers. I don't know why there is so much hype about the *'terrible twos'* (and I don't wish to know, thank you) but I wasn't warned about the *'woeful ones'*. Yes yes, her language is developing and she's becoming independent and it's miraculous, but come on, how am I meant to reason with a child who loses her shit because I won't let her eat a used tampon? How do you rationally explain to a one-year old that, despite its exciting exterior and similar name, the toilet brush is riddled with faeces and not a suitable toothbrush alternative? And how the fuck do you reason with a flailing little devil in the packed aisles of *ASDA,* who is beyond furious that you've fought to stop her smashing a £19 bottle of pinot grigio on the floor?

She recently staged her first *leaving home* protest, all because I stopped her from sucking the contents out of a tube of *E45.* She took her blanket and a drink into her tepee, and refused to leave until I had met her irrational demands. As it happens, I recall that afternoon as one of the greatest of my life; I decided not to barter with her, left her to it and watched re-runs of *The Apprentice.* On. My. Own.

The worst bit of a tantrum is undoubtedly that vile ability to simultaneously stop the function of all of their limbs, so they hang lifeless in your arms like a useless pack of shit, flopping their legs as they hit the ground to prevent themselves from standing. To be even more of an Isabellend, she throws her head back too, so if you're not careful, she will indefinitely smash her own bonce onto the floor, giving her a real reason to cry, which, will undoubtedly be my fault.

Oh, how I remember my *Hypothetical Mum* days; watching on at hapless parents, tutting at their incompetence and revelling in the thoughts that my child would never, ever behave this way, especially not in public.

Let's all just laugh at that for a minute. Then cry.

I don't deserve this, I've worked hard, loved my family and sometimes I even donate to charity. Why did I end up with the pissed army general barking orders at me like I'm her snack bitch? Why is my child the one ordered off *Wish,* that looks and functions nothing like the advert? I genuinely thought that I'd have the magic touch; this innate ability to calm her, reason with her and prevent a tantrum from ever occurring. I foolishly thought that those mothers in the supermarket, with the feral child smashing their head against the trolley, was all down to their poor attempts at parenting. Bless my innocence, and get me a gin.

Teething

Ah, that shit show cranks up a notch in year two, doesn't it? I thought that those teeny incisors were nasty, but molars take the biscuit.

However, I have found a golden nugget. It may have only taken 16 teeth and over 140 sleepless nights, but I've finally discovered the magic of *Ashton and Parsons* teething powder. It's like crack for kids. Whack a bit of that in her mouth and the incessant screaming stops immediately. I mean, I have no idea what's actually in it, or how much to put on, but the crying stops. Not sure her face is meant to go numb, though?

Television

Look, we've got to talk about *Pat*. I didn't want to drop him in it but he's tampering with mail in almost every episode, and it's illegal. What would Queen Lizzy say if she knew that her postal service was not only performing sub-optimally, but her special deliveries are taking at least half a day longer to arrive to their unsuspecting recipients, all because *Pat* the postie can't stop snooping in the parcels. It's outrageous. I'm also suspicious about his requirement for a fleet of vehicles, which all have personalised registration plates by the way. I thought he was a sole trader? I'm sure he's on some kind of tax avoidance scheme.

And don't get me started on that creepy little panda in *Bing*, who, for no reason whatsoever, takes his pants off in the opening sequence of the show. Look mate, you can't just run down the street and whip your arse out, endangered or not. And for the ones who are saying *'it's wonderful, it unites children who, when excitable, remove their clothes'.* No, it doesn't. But what it does do it teach my monster that she too can remove her pants, in *Tesco.* Thanks.

I've also got to mention the unrealistic expectations set out by *Thomas and Friends* of our country's *National Rail Service.* Apparently, he can travel the world on one single track, and yet, I can't get a direct train from Liverpool to Newcastle.

To be honest, I think all of this pent-up anger is misdirected. I'm actually just really confused. For the first half of this year, I begged for her to be interested in the TV, willing to sacrifice her teeny-little brain cells and burn *CBeebies* into her retinas, but she wasn't interested. Now, she's obsessed with the TV, demanding *'Oh Doddy'* and his squirrel friends, or that satanic little prick, *Peppa.* I can't stand that programme. It makes me motion sick when they make the screen shake, and I genuinely feel enraged when they all ROFL. Nobody's done that since 2007.

THANKLESS

When is she going to acknowledge all the hard work that I'm putting in to keep her alive? It's a bitch just trying to get her to say *'thanks'* for a biscuit. Some days, I feel like I've done a bloody glorious job of feeding, clothing and generally not killing her, and what do I get in return? A half-chewed sausage roll and her snot wiped on the sleeve of my hoodie.

Tidy-up time

Seriously, what is the fucking point? The mum books tell you to *'keep the chaos under control by having a designated play area'.* Yeah, right. I look back now at the foolish, pathetically-naïve pregnant woman standing in my living room, saying *'we can just keep all of her stuff in the playroom and keep in here for us'.* Oh, how we laughed, what a silly little woman I was.

Yesterday, I found three wooden ducks in the washing machine. I guess this is where they go when they swim *over the hill and far away.* Poor sods were sloshing around in there on a hot wash with my work uniform, I'm surprised that they didn't come out as eggs again.

I've often had zoom meetings with half of Old McDonald's livestock in the background. I've found Elsa's shoe in the fridge, and had half a week's worth of wooden shopping in my sock drawer. I'm not even sure how it gets there, she's like a stealth smuggler of shit from room to room, making her sticky little mark on every square foot of my house.

I think it's time that I finally accepted it; our home is going to be rocking the post-Hiroshima vibes for the next few years.

TIME

Toddlers live within a different time zone. In fact, their concept of time is so farcically out of sync with the rest of the world that it makes me want to ram the hands of my watch into my eyeballs, so that I never get to see how late I'm running ever again.

Gina Ford told me (in the stern voice that I read her book in my head in) that children don't understand the concept of time until they are three. But they can lose their shit because I'm taking too long in the post office queue. Go figure.

Pre-child life must have been a parallel universe, in which time meant something completely different to me, too. The same as tiredness. I remember my 22-year old self constantly complaining to my new-mum colleagues that I was tired, because I'd had seven and a half hours sleep rather than eight. God, they must have thought I was a prick.

Looking back now, I have to wonder what I filled my child-free time with. I'd get home from work at 4.35pm and stay up until at least 10.30pm. That's six hours of fuckallness. I bet I hoovered behind the bed in those days. Maybe even cleaned the car. I bet I showered daily. Ah, memories.

There is something rather odd about looking back to a life before Isabelle. In a way, it feels like she's been here forever, and though I know that Danny and I had 12 years together before her, I can't imagine it being just us two now.

God, what the hell would we talk about?

Toothbrushing

These bastards have caused me nothing but trouble since their arrival. From sleepless nights to screaming out in pain, her teeth have been a nightmare from the very first bulge. And now, even though they're going to fall out despite what I do, I'm obliged to clean them, twice daily. Of course, that wouldn't be a problem if they were left on the side like dentures, and not in the mouth of a savage toddler.

I'm not sure if you've ever wrestled open the snappy orifice of a child, but it's a tremendous pain in the arse. Somehow, she manages to scream incessantly, without actually opening her mouth enough to sneak a brush in. Surely pinning and straddling a child in an attempt to preserve teeth that will inevitably surrender in a couple of years is utterly pointless? I've tried letting her brush my teeth, and singing those god-awful toothy songs, but she's not for budging. I'd say it's alright because she doesn't eat sugar, but that high-horse, *Hypothetical Mum* standard fucked off a long time ago.

I thought I'd cracked it when one day, Miss Independent asked for her toothbrush when I was brushing my teeth. But no, she just sucked the water off and then threw it in the toilet. Well, that's me told.

So, please, if you have any suggestions, write in to denturesby5@gmail.com.

U

UH-OH

The utterance she declares immediately after throwing her dinner/a dolly/herself on the floor. It's usually accompanied by a sarcastic *'oh, what happened?'* hand gesture, and a wry smile. The little shit.

Understanding

It still blows my mind that the puffy, purple alien that they cut out of me in 2019 can now follow instructions to *'go and get your shoes'* or *'give Mickey Mouse some banana'* (one of these instructions is infinitely more useful than the other, but they're equally as cute when followed).

What isn't so cute is when they understand what you're saying, but choose not to hear it. Like when you politely request that they *don't put dolly's head in the toilet'* or *'come here quickly before you wee on the floor'.* And I thought that she didn't have her father's personality...

V

Velcro

It's a clever little idea *Velcro;* stick-stick and get on with your day, without a lace in sight. The problem is, kids find it fucking fascinating. If you lower the radio during a car journey (to *'see better',* of course), you will inevitably hear the sticking and unsticking of a toddler's shoe, which isn't a problem until you've arrived at your destination and find one shoe's gone AWOL amongst the half-eaten snack packets and the discarded, headless dolls that live in the footwell.

It wouldn't be a problem if your darling was still a babe in arms, but now, Miss Independent can, and must, walk. So, we fish for the shoe, invariably fingering the goo of a mouldy strawberry that's festering just out of reach. Five stress-filled minutes pass, before said child proudly presents the shoe that she's been holding all along, which managed to stick itself to the inside of the fleecy jacket she's wearing, instead of the coat I wanted her to wear, but couldn't because of the bastard rules on coats in car seats. Fucking *Velcro*.

VIRAL RASHES

The deep-rooted fear of meningitis is instilled in every parent. And if you've ever had a child with a rash, you'll know the pit-of-the-stomach sicky feeling that those teeny little bumps can cause. I, for one, have spent many a night rolling a glass by torchlight onto Isabelle's sleeping limbs; googling and re-googling what *'blanching'* and *'non-blanching'* mean. It's terrifying.

Doctors, on the other hand, don't find these rashes scary at all. In fact, they could pretty much smell a rash and they'd call it *'viral'.* It's insane. My Mum doesn't remember me ever getting a rash as a baby, but, apparently, they're really common in one-year olds who have swam in that petri-dish called *nursery.* Unless you're a dermatologist, they all look the bloody same, so you're guaranteed to spend at least a week's worth of nights in the out of hours, because even though you know they're going to say *'it's viral',* you couldn't live with the guilt of getting it wrong.

As a parenting rite of passage, or, more likely, a ploy from the GP to stop me mithering him, the last time we went, the doctor asked me to get a water sample from her. You know, my incontinent one-year old who won't sit still for longer than 15 seconds. It took me five attempts to capture enough piss, leaving both Isabelle and I utterly traumatised, and my front room was like a slip 'n' slide in a nursing home. And the result?

Viral infection.

VISITORS

Almost two years in and I've finally mastered leaving the house with a child. The problem is, nobody will take us, and if I'm honest, I'd rather shit in my hands and clap than take my whirling ball of destruction into someone else's home. It takes at least 20 minutes to clear the ornaments out of her reach in Granny's house, and somehow, my tornado toddler still manages to find the one porcelain heirloom that we had missed and teeter it dangerously close to the edge of a table. My heart is in my mouth the entire visit.

If it's a home I don't know myself, or one that's definitely not Izzy-proofed, then the panic cranks up a level; she'll disappear out of sight within the blink of an eye, and reappear holding the hostess' dirty underwear from the washing machine, or a glass photoframe of their dead relative.

I think we're going to have to hibernate until she's 18.

WEIRDOS

Toddlers are so weird. I guess you could say they're *liberated:* free from the conforms of daily life and societal pressures, which, when you say it like that, sounds bloody glorious. But when you're their mum, who sadly isn't even free to shit in peace, it's a ruddy pain in the backside.

In the past, we've had to abandon shopping trolleys because Isabelle wouldn't take a storage box off her head in *B&M*, and kept running into the groins of other people. *'Control your child'* I can here Karen say, but frankly, I'd have more luck mediating discussions between North and South Korea.

I just don't get why they have to do irritating things. Like, why does she find it too damn mainstream to sit on the couch in the conventional manner? Why, particularly when she's eating, does she need to hang off the back of it like Miley Cyrus on her wrecking ball?

Why does she continually want to climb the stairs and then, at the top, turn around at rapid pace, scaring the shit out of her poor mother?

I don't even think it's just that she has no sense of danger (though I will add that to the list of things that I need to get around to teaching her), I think they just like being a bit odd; always testing the water for a reaction.

She's such a performer and loves to try to make us laugh at her expense (OK, maybe she is a bit like me, too). Like, she's started putting her tissues down her top (thanks Grandma) and every so often she whips it out and says 'ta-da!' then claps. It's hilarious, but I definitely couldn't get away with it myself.

On a recent shopping trip, she randomly shouted *'FIRE!'*. Every shopper in the vicinity shat themselves. There was no fire.

WIT WOO

Whenever Isabelle would get into the bath at her Grandma's, Danny's Mum would say *'wit woo'* to her little nakey bum. We naïvely didn't think that it would escalate to her hollering *'wit woo'* every time her Mummy or Daddy would get their kit off. This morning, I showered whilst she was in the bath beneath me. She pretty much wolf-whistled at me for the duration of my wash; it worked wonders for my body confidence!

It doesn't have the same effect when Daddy strips off though, there's definitely something *Saville* about our kid whooping over her Dad's bare arse. Though, I guess it's better than those couple of months when she used to just point and laugh at him. Poor Daddy.

WORK

After over 12 months of leggings and mum buns, I was ready to dive back into working life, as Isabelle approached her first birthday. I'm not going to lie, the thought of setting a 6.30am alarm after a year of broken sleep wasn't thrilling, but realising my potential, beyond cutting grapes into quarters and replicating the *Hot Dog dance*, was an exciting prospect.

Before Isabelle was born, I headed up the Stroke Speech Therapy service at our hospital. I had always loved people management, service development and maximising the quality of care for our patients, but as the day loomed, I doubted my knowledge and my ability to balance life as a *Mum Boss*. I had planned on working almost full-time hours – how on earth would I fit that into my parenting schedule? And who the fuck would clean the house?

As it happens, I don't mind being a busy bee. The structure and routine of returning to work gave my week a focus; a timetable with which I'd fit my life around. Of course, the *mum guilt* is there: am I not spending enough time with her? Will she resent me for never being around, or will she grow up in awe of her Mama who climbed to the top and held on tight, whilst juggling 20 different balls of life? I spend every Thursday with her, and every other

Tuesday, and somehow, it works. Some days, I drop the balls (mainly the *'Good Wife'* one, but that's rubber, so it bounces back in time).

Interestingly, my need to work was greater than I'd expected. I thrive on accomplishment, productivity and success, and, though my daughter provides me with multiple challenges a day, the mundanity of repeatedly cleaning toothpaste off the bathroom door handle, or picking raisins out from down the back of the sofa, weren't challenging me in the ways I'd hoped.

Returning to an intellectually-challenging environment made me a better mum. There, I've said it. I appreciate our time together so much more when I've been and *'done me'.* And though the bags under my eyes may suggest otherwise, there is nothing more glorious than that snuggle at the nursery pick-up after a long day on the wards.

So, I guess if you're due to go back from mat leave anytime soon, know that *it's ok.* Yes, you've always got one ear out for your phone in case nursery ring and say she's chopped a limb off, but it hasn't happened, yet. And anyway, surely I'm paying them enough to sew it back on.

X

Xylophone

This pisses me off. I'm trying to teach my kid the alphabet, and every song seems to think that the most appropriate word to use for X is *xylophone*. You know, the word that nobody ever fucking says, and that doesn't even begin with an *'ex'* sound.

And before you start, I also think *x-ray* is a cop-out; what kind of desperate, last-ditch book-writing attempt (other than mine) uses the following categories together, *'animal, animal, toy, item of clothing, animal, radiography procedure'.* It's random AF.

Y

I know I'm cheating by putting the *'why'* section here, but let's be honest, no-one is paying attention to the formatting at this stage of the game. And don't pretend that you care, you've never put in as much effort teaching the end of the alphabet as you did at the start.

So, here we go. *WHY? Why, why, why? Why do I need to go to bed? Why do I need to wear pants? Why did Mummy and Daddy think it was a good idea to pro-create and not just buy that second home on the Greek Isles?*

It's pretty insane when you realise that you are turning into your own mother. I love my mum to bits, and genuinely think that there is nobody I'd rather be like, but, there is nothing more ageing than the moment you start saying things like, *'because I said so'.* and *'because it's the rules'* (as if there is a fluffing rule book somewhere that tells us what to do - *Gina Ford*, I'm looking at you).

YOU

Here's an excerpt from the chapter of the same title, taken from the first book:

Nobody told me that I would lose myself. That some days I'd crave my old life and all that came with it. That I'd miss the spontaneity, the freedom and my sense of self. That I'd even miss going to work. Then the mum guilt hits.

How could I possibly grieve for my old life when I'm meant to be so overwhelmingly besotted with my new, shiny, shit-stained one? People would give anything for the gift of a child, I know, I've been right there in the fertility clinic with the best of them.

But in amongst that infinite love and absolute joy was a little twinge of sadness as I realised that my life has changed immeasurably. Some days, even still, I find it sad that I can't run off to New Zealand to do my PhD, or do another summer working at Disney World. And though Insta Mamas suggest that you 'still can', I'm not sure it'd be the same on 3 hours sleep and a tiny person sucking on your nipples.

I've also changed as a wife. My priority isn't Danny anymore. He isn't my number one. And just writing that makes me cry. I'm too exhausted to make an effort anymore. I snap at him for the smallest of *things because I spend all day in the damn shithole of a house – which no matter how often you clean still ends up a bomb site – or surrounded by mums who are just fucking boring.*

For the first few months of Isabelle's life, I think we just existed. We survived day-by-day and our communication was purely based around what time the new tenant had woken, fed or shat. I lived on auto-mum mode until I reached breaking point when she was about 3 and a half months old. I couldn't be this baby feeding robot anymore. She would scream constantly and I would cry right alongside her. I wanted out. Not out of her life, just out of the house without a massive bag full of baby shit. Just a shower on my own. Just one full night's sleep.

So, I contacted work and asked if I could do a couple of Keeping in Touch (KIT) days. I contacted my friends and asked them to meet up for tea; without the kids. And I told Danny I needed him at home more.

It wasn't me failing, it was me recognising that I needed to find me again. I love being Mum, but I love it even more when I'm refreshed after a little break. Nobody tells you it's OK to want a break from your kids. Maybe a screaming toddler or a moody-ass teenager. But not a newborn.

But here I was searching for breathing space away from the snuggles of a teeny helpless little person. Not because I didn't love her, but because I remembered that I needed to still love me.

It's still difficult to read those words back. I want to grab that new mama and tell her *'it will be ok'.* I want to hold her, pour her a gin and tell her about all the wonderful things that are to come. I want her to know that that little baby will grow into the strong-willed, independent and funny little Isabelle that I know now. I want to tell her that nobody gives a shit that your house is up the wall, and that her and Danny will be ok.

Importantly, I want her to know that needing a break isn't a luxury, it's a necessity. Being a mum isn't a sprint, it's a shit tonne of marathons, and you start them without ever having set foot on a treadmill. That breather is sometimes your only way to survive the next mile.

Looking at who I've become now, I'm a far cry from the girl in book one, but I'm still trying to find my feet every single day. I still have to accept parcels through the window because I've lost my key, my body still looks like it needs an iron, and I still don't have a clue what I'm doing. But, I've stopped reflecting on all of the things I can't do, and I've started exploring some of the things that I still can, like a masters degree, a long bath after bedtime, and time away with the girls.

Have I figured out motherhood? No. But who has? Some days, I feel like a batch-cooking, game-playing, bedding-washing mother-fluffer, and others, I settle with a chippy and back-to-back *Peppa*. Because, like anything, it's all about balance. The slob days allow me to recharge my batteries, ready for the next day. This motherhood thing is here for the long haul, and even a concord wouldn't reach its destination without a refuel.

So, who am I now?

I'm Bex, a reluctant adult who is winging it with the best of them. And you know what? I'm doing just fine.

(What a beautiful end to the book. Oh, fuck, we've not done *Z*. Hang on, just a few more pages).

Z

Zoo

Remember pre-parenthood when you'd hypothetically plan days out to the zoo? You'd imagine these gorgeous little trips full of educational interaction and flooded with new language, a picnic by the giraffes and maybe a little treat from the gift shop at the end. Well, as it turns out, one-year olds don't care about the zoo. They enjoy picking stones up from the floor in the zoo, or running away from you in the zoo, but they're not too fussed about the constitutional parts that actually make a zoo a zoo. Like the animals. She couldn't give two fucks that that's a zebra, there is a dead spider on the fence. She's not arsed one bit about the baby orangutan that we've queued for 20 minutes to see, because that leaf has bird poo on it. The only time that she gives a flying crap that we've been to the zoo is on the way out, through that bastard gift shop. Then, and only then, is it paramount that we celebrate our zoo trip by purchasing a huge lion, despite not caring in the slightest about the real-life lion that we've just travelled 45 minutes to see. Give me strength.

ZOOM

Remember a time before fucking *Zoom?* Nah, me neither. I knew Covid would sneak it's way in there somehow.

Thank you

Wow. This has been a pretty crazy year. I released the first book in the midst of a global pandemic, and somehow, it reached a number one best-seller in the charts, through online growth alone.

I appreciate the support more than you'll ever know, and want to take the time to thank a few people who have made it happen (I know this bit is usually really boring but I'll try and jazz it up a bit):

-   Thank you to all the podcasts who had me on as a guest; you took a punt on me and I really appreciate it. There truly is nothing better than a gaggle of mothers coming together to have a mutual rant about their kids.

- Thank you to my *tribe* on Instagram; who have continued to like my stupid posts about Isabelle's crazy hair or my ridiculous parenting meltdowns. In the online world, rightly or wrongly, so much rides on the number of Insta followers you have, so I really appreciate you sticking around.

- Thanks to *Stacey Duncan*, the world's greatest friend, nurse and grammar police officer. Also to *Becs Jeffrey*, a phenomenal copywriter (@becs.writes.and.wears) and the co-creator of the BEST parenting clothing brand out there (@Jugglewear).

- Thanks to everyone who has looked after Isabelle while I've zoomed, recorded, Insta-lived and written. I know how insane I am to try and do this alongside my almost full-time job and full-time Mum life, and you've made it so much easier. Particularly our wonderful family, you don't know how much I love you.

- Finally, thanks to every single person who bought this book. You're supporting a dream. That sounds ridiculously lame, and it is, but it's true.

And finally, please, please, please review the book on Amazon (only if you liked it, of course. If you didn't, then say absolutely nothing – literally, *Mum's the Word*). The reviews make ALL the difference, and I genuinely do a happy dance when I see a nice one. Also, come and say hello on the socials, particularly Instagram (unless you're an Amazon seller, pushy MLMer or person who opens a generic DM with *'Hey lovely'* or *'Hi Hun'*):

@BOOKMUMSTHEWORD

PS I'm still waiting on that en suite

Printed in Great Britain
by Amazon